Demonology

King James I

Filiquarian Publishing, LLC is publishing this edition of Demonology, due to its public domain status.

The cover design of this edition of Demonology is copyright 2006, Filiquarian Publishing, LLC.

Filiquarian Publishing, LLC

Contents

King James I

Introduction

The Dæmonologie of King James, the Sixth of Scotland and First of England, was written, as the Royal author states in his Preface, to prove that 'the assautes of Sathan are most certainly practized, & that the instrumentes thereof, merits most severly to be punished.' Such a work has more than a passing interest. It gives the student of history and literature a brief and authoritative guide to the darker beliefs of our ancestors; there is, too, much to interest the theologian and the psychologist, whilst the philologist will find the book a mine of rare and curious phrases.

To the modern mind, after three centuries of scientific discovery, many of Epistemon's arguments will appear somewhat naïve, and, it must be confessed, that Philomathes, in his laudable efforts to draw out his companion's erudition, sometimes puts questions which are very inadequately answered. Our greater discernment and weaker faith will scarcely be convinced by the example: 'Thirdly, said not Samuell to Saull, that disobedience is as the sinne of Witch-craft? To compare to a thing that were not, it were too too absurd.' Still, given the implicit belief, the conclusions are not illogical. King James makes many shrewd observations, and the twentieth-century medium would probably confirm 'that there are twentie women giuen to that craft, where ther is one man.' The explanation would not, perhaps, be as readily accepted.

The Newes from Scotland, which is also included in this volume of the Bodley Head Quartos, claims to give a true account of a very notable witch trial wherein King James took a prominent part. The influence of the 'revelations' then made can clearly be seen in the Dæmonologie. Although at first sight the cruelty and barbarity of the whole business is revolting, it must not be put down as solely due to panic and terror. These poor women when their heads were 'thrawen with a rope according to the custom of that Country' were ready to confess anything, but the credulity of the judges was understandable after Agnis Sampson had drawn the King aside and 'declared vnto him the verye woordes which passed betweene the Kings Maiestie and his Queene at Vpslo in Norway the first night of their marriage, with their answere each to other.' Even a stouter hearted scholar would have found remarkable confirmation of his worst fears in this alarming revelation. Moreover, in destroying the Devil's ministers the King really thought that he was only carrying out his plain duty towards God.

Of King James himself one of the most vivid accounts is to be found in a letter of Sir John Harrington, describing an audience which he had with the King. 'Soon upon this, the Prince his Highnesse did enter, and in muche goode humour askede, "If I was cosen to lorde Haryngton of Exton?" I humblie repliede,-- "His Majestie did me some honour in enquiringe my kin to one whome he had so late honourede and made a barone;" and moreover did adde, "wee were bothe branches of the same tree." The he enquyrede muche of lernynge, and showede me his owne in suche sorte, as made me remember my examiner at Cambridge aforetyme. He soughte muche to knowe my advances in philosophie, and utterede profounde sentences of Aristotle, and suche lyke wryters, whiche I had never reade, and which some are bolde enoughe to saye, others do not understand: but this I must passe by. The Prince did nowe presse my readinge to him parte of a canto in "Ariosto";

6

praysede my utterance, and said he had been informede of manie, as to my lernynge, in the tyme of the Queene. He asked me "what I thought pure witte was made of; and whom it did best become? Whether a Kynge should not be the best clerke in his owne countrie; and, if this lande did not entertayne goode opinion of his lernynge and wisdome?" His Majestie did much presse for my opinion touchinge the power of Satane in matter of witchcraft; and asked me, with much gravitie,--"if I did trulie understande, why the devil did worke more with anciente women than others?"' . .

'More serious discourse did next ensue, wherein I wantede roome to continue, and sometime roome to escape; for the Queene was not forgotten, nor Davison neither. His Highnesse tolde me her deathe was visible in Scotlande before it did really happen, being, as he said, "spoken of in secrete by those whose power of sighte presentede to them a bloodie heade dancinge in the aire." He then did remarke muche on this gifte, and saide he had soughte out of certaine bookes a sure waie to attaine knowledge of future chances. Hereat, he namede many bookes, which I did not knowe, nor by whom written; but advisede me not to consult some authors which woulde leade me to evile consultations. I tolde his Majestie, "the power of Satan had, I muche fearede, damagede my bodilie frame; but I had not farther will to cowrte his friendshipe, for my soules hurt."--We nexte discoursede somewhat on religion, when at lengthe he saide: "Now, Sir, you have seen my wisdome in some sorte, and I have pried into yours. I praye you, do me justice in your reporte, and in good season, I will not fail to add to your understandinge, in suche pointes as I maye find you lacke amendmente." I made courtesie hereat, and withdrewe downe the passage, and out at the gate, amidst the manie varlets and lordlie servantes who stoode arounde.'[1]

7

G. B. HARRISON

[1. Nugae Antiquae, i 367.]

Preface

The Preface to the Reader.

The fearefull aboundinge at this time in this countrie, of these detestable slaues of the Deuill, the Witches or enchaunters, hath moved me (beloued reader) to dispatch in post, this following treatise of mine, not in any wise (as I protest) to serue for a shew of my learning & ingine, but onely (mooued of conscience) to preasse / thereby, so farre as I can, to resolue the doubting harts of many; both that such assaultes of Sathan are most certainly practized, & that the instrumentes thereof, merits most severly to be punished: against the damnable opinions of two principally in our age, wherof the one called SCOT an Englishman, is not ashamed in publike print to deny, that ther can be such a thing as Witch-craft: and so mainteines the old error of the Sadducees, in denying of spirits. The other called VVIERVS, a German Phisition, sets out a publick apologie for al these craftesfolkes, whereby, procuring for their impunitie, he plainely bewrayes himselfe to haue bene one of that Profession. And for to make this treatise the more pleasaunt and facill, I haue put it in forme of a Dialogue, which I haue diuided into three bookes: The first spea- / king of Magie in general, and Necromancie in special. The second of Sorcerie and Witch-craft: and the thirde, conteines a discourse of all these kindes of spirits, & Spectres that appeares & trobles persones: together with a conclusion of the whol work. My intention in this labour, is only to proue two things, as I haue alreadie said: the one, that such diuelish artes haue bene and are. The other, what exact trial and seuere punishment they merite: & therefore reason I, what kinde of things are possible

to be performed in these arts, & by what naturall causes they
may be, not that I touch every particular thing of the Deuils
power, for that were infinite: but onelie, to speak scholasticklie,
(since this can not bee spoken in our language) I reason vpon
genus leauing species, and differentia to be comprehended
therein. / As for example, speaking of the power of Magiciens,
in the first book & sixt Chapter: I say, that they can suddenly
cause be brought vnto them, all kindes of daintie disshes, by
their familiar spirit: Since as a thiefe he delightes to steale, and
as a spirite, he can subtillie & suddenlie inough transport the
same. Now vnder this genus, may be comprehended al
particulars, depending thereupon; Such as the bringing Wine
out of a Wall, (as we haue heard oft to haue bene practised) and
such others; which particulars, are sufficientlie proued by the
reasons of the general. And such like in the second booke of
Witch-craft in speciall, and fift Chap. I say and proue by
diuerse arguments, that Witches can, by the power of their
Master, cure or cast on disseases: Now by these same reasones,
that proues their power by the / Deuil of disseases in generall,
is aswell proued their power in speciall: as of weakening the
nature of some men, to make them vnable for women: and
making it to abound in others, more then the ordinary course of
nature would permit. And such like in all other particular
sicknesses; But one thing I will pray thee to obserue in all these
places, where I reason vpon the deuils power, which is the
diferent ends & scopes, that God as the first cause, and the
Devill as his instrument and second cause shootes at in all
these actiones of the Deuil, (as Gods hang-man:) For where the
deuilles intention in them is euer to perish, either the soule or
the body, or both of them, that he is so permitted to deale with:
God by the contrarie, drawes euer out of that euill glorie to
himselfe, either by the wracke of the wicked in his justice, or /
by the tryall of the patient, and amendment of the faithfull,

being wakened vp with that rod of correction. Hauing thus
declared vnto thee then, my full intention in this Treatise, thou
wilt easelie excuse, I doubt not, aswel my pretermitting, to
declare the whole particular rites and secretes of these
vnlawfull artes: as also their infinite and wounderfull practises,
as being neither of them pertinent to my purpose: the reason
whereof, is giuen in the hinder ende of the first Chapter of the
thirde booke: and who likes to be curious in these thinges, he
may reade, if he will here of their practises, BODINVS
Dæmonomanie, collected with greater diligence, then written
with judgement, together with their confessions, that haue bene
at this time apprehened. If he would know what hath bene the
opinion of the Aunci- / entes, concerning their power: he shall
see it wel descrybed by HYPERIVS, & HEMMINGIVS, two,
late Germaine writers: Besides innumerable other neoterick
Theologues, that writes largelie vpon that subject: And if he
woulde knowe what are the particuler rites, & curiosities of
these black arts (which is both vnnecessarie and perilous,) he
will finde it in the fourth book of CORNELIVS Agrippa, and
in VVIERVS, whomof spak. And so wishing my pains in this
Treatise (beloued Reader) to be effectual, in arming al them
that reades the same, against these aboue mentioned erroures,
and recommending my goodwill to thy friendly acceptation, I
bid thee hartely fare-well.

JAMES R.

King James I

Dæmonologie

The First Booke

CHAP. I. ARGVMENT.

Proven by the Scripture, that these vnlawfull artes in genere, have bene and may be put in practise.

PHILOMATHES and EPISTEMON reason the matter.

PHILOMATHES.

I AM surely verie glad to haue mette with you this daye, for I am of opinion, that ye can better resolue me of some thing, wherof I stand in great doubt, nor anie other whom-with I could haue mette.

EPI. In what I can, that ye like to speir at me, I will willinglie and freelie tell my opinion, and if I proue it not sufficiently, I am heartely content that a better reason carie it away then.

PHI. What thinke yee of these strange newes, which now onelie furnishes purpose to al men at their meeting: I meane of these Witches?

EPI. Surelie they are wonderfull: And I think so cleare and plaine confessions in that purpose, haue neuer fallen out in anie age or cuntrey.

PHI. No question if they be true, but thereof the Doctours doubtes.

EPI. What part of it doubt ye of?

PHI. Even of all, for ought I can yet perceaue: and namelie, that there is such a thing as Witchcraft or Witches, and I would pray you to resolue me thereof if ye may: for I haue reasoned with sundrie in that matter, and yet could never be satisfied therein.

EPI. I shall with good will doe the best I can: But I thinke it the difficiller, since ye denie the thing it selfe in generall: for as it is said in the logick schools, Contra negantem principia non est disputandum. Alwaies for that part, that witchcraft, and Witches haue bene, and are, the former part is clearelie proved b the Scriptures, and the last by dailie experience and confessions.

PHI. I know Yee will alleadge me Saules Pythonisse: but that as appeares will not make much for you.

EPI. Not onlie that place, but divers others: But I marvel why that should not make much for me?

PHI. The reasones are these, first Yee may consider, that Saul[1. 1. Sam. 28.] being troubled in spirit, and having fasted long before, as the text testifieth, and being come to a woman that was bruted to have such knowledge, and that to inquire so important news, he having so guiltie a conscience for his hainous offences, and specially, for that same vnlawful curiositie, and horrible defection: and then the woman crying out vpon the suddaine in great admiration, for the vncouth sicht that she alledged to haue sene, discovering him to be the King, thogh disguysed, & denied by him before: it was no wounder I say, that his senses being thus distracted, he could not perceaue hir faining of hir voice, hee being himselfe in an other chalmer, and seeing nothing. Next what could be, or was raised? The spirit of Samuel? Prophane and against all Theologie: the Diuell in his likenes? as vnappeirant, that either God would permit him to come in the shape of his Saintes (for then could neuer the Prophets in those daies haue bene sure, what Spirit spake to them in their visiones) or then that he could fore-tell what was to come there after; for Prophecie proceedeth onelie of G O D: and the Devill hath no knowledge of things to come.

EPI. Yet if Yee will marke the wordes of the text, ye will finde clearely, that Saul saw that apparition: for giving you that Saul was in an other Chalmer, at the making of the circles & conjurationes, needeful for that purpose (as none of that craft will permit any vthers to behold at that time) yet it is evident by the text, that how sone that once that vnclean spirit was fully risen, shee called in vpon Saul. For it is saide in the text, that Saule knew him to be Samuel, which coulde not haue bene, by the hearing tell onely of an olde man with an mantil, since there was many mo old men dead in Israel nor Samuel: And the common weid of that whole Cuntrey was mantils. As to the next, that it was not the spirit of Samuel, I grant: In the proving whereof ye neede not to insist, since all Christians of whatso-ever Religion agrees vpon that: and none but either mere ignorants, or Necromanciers or Witches doubtes thereof. And that the Diuel is permitted at som-times to put himself in the liknes of the Saintes, it is plaine in the Scriptures, where it is said, that Sathan can trans-forme himselfe into an Angell of light[1. 2. Cor. 11. 14.]. Neither could that bring any inconvenient with the visiones of the Prophets, since it is most certaine, that God will not permit him so to deceiue his own: but only such, as first wilfully deceiues them-selves, by running vnto him, whome God then suffers to fall in their owne snares, and justlie permittes them to be illuded with great efficacy of deceit, because they would not beleeue the trueth (as Paul sayth). And as to the diuelles foretelling of things to come, it is true that he knowes not all things future, but yet that he knowes parte, the Tragicall event of this historie declares it, (which the wit of woman could never haue fore-spoken) not that he hath any prescience, which is only proper to God: or yet knows anie thing by loking vpon God, as in a mirrour (as the good Angels doe) he being for euer debarred from the fauorable presence & countenance of his creator, but only by one of these two meanes, either as being worldlie wise, and taught by an continuall experience, ever since the creation, judges by likelie-hood of thinges to come, according to the like that hath passed before, and the naturall causes, in respect of the vicissitude of all thinges; worldly: Or else by Gods employing of him in a turne, and so foreseene thereof: as appeares to haue bin in this, whereof we finde the verie like in Micheas propheticque discourse to King Achab[1. 1. King. 22]. But to prooue this my first proposition, that there can be such a thing as witch-craft, & witches, there are manie mo places in the Scriptures then this (as I said before). As first in the law of God, it is plainely prohibited[2. Exod. 22]: But certaine it is, that the Law of God speakes nothing in vaine, nether doth it lay curses, or injoyne punishmentes vpon shaddowes, condemning that to be il, which is not in essence or being as we call it. Secondlie it is plaine, where wicked Pharaohs wise-men imitated ane number of Moses miracles[3. Exod. 7 & 8], to harden the tyrants heart there by. Thirdly, said not Samuell to Saull, that disobedience is as the sinne of Witch-craft?[4. 1.

Sam. 15] To compare to a thing that were not, it were too too absurd. Fourthlie, was not Simon Magus, a man of that craft? And fiftlie, what was she that had the spirit of Python?[5. Acts. 8] beside innumerable other places that were irkesom to recite.

CHAP. II. ARGV.

What kyndie of sin the practizers of these vnlawfull artes committes. The division of these artes. And quhat are the meanes that allures any to practize them.

PHILOMATHES.

BVT I thinke it very strange, that God should permit anie man-kynde (since they beare his owne Image) to fall in so grosse and filthie a defection.

EPI. Although man in his Creation was made to the Image of the Creator[1. Gen. 1.], yet through his fall having once lost it, it is but restored againe in a part by grace onelie to the elect: So all the rest falling away from God, are given over in the handes of the Devill that enemie, to beare his Image: and being once so given over, the greatest and the grossest impietie, is the pleasantest, and most delytefull vnto them.

PHI. But may it not suffice him to haue indirectly the rule, and procure the perdition of so manie soules by alluring them to vices, and to the following of their own appetites, suppose he abuse not so many simple soules, in making them directlie acknowledge him for their maister.

EPI. No surelie, for hee vses everie man, whom of he hath the rule, according to their complexion and knowledge: And so whome he findes most simple, he plaineliest discovers himselfe vnto them. For hee beeing the enemie of mans Salvation, vses al the meanes he can to entrappe them so farre in his snares, as it may be vnable to them thereafter (suppose they would) to rid themselues out of the same.

PHI. Then this sinne is a sinne against the holie Ghost.

EPI. It is in some, but not in all.

PHI. How that? Are not all these that runnes directlie to the Devill in one Categorie.

EPI. God forbid, for the sin against the holie Ghost hath two branches: The one a falling backe from the whole service of G O D, and a refusall of all his preceptes. The other is the doing of the first with knowledge, knowing that they doe wrong against their own conscience, and the testimonie of the holie Spirit, having once had a tast of the sweetnes of Gods mercies[1. Heb. 6.]. Now in the first of these two, all sortes of Necromancers, Enchanters or Witches, ar comprehended: but in the last, none but such as erres with this knowledge that I haue spoken of.

PHI Then it appeares that there are more sortes nor one, that are directlie professors of his service: and if so be, I pray you tell me how manie, and what are they?

EPI. There are principallie two sortes, wherevnto all the partes of that vnhappie arte are redacted; whereof the one is called Magie or Necromancie, the other Sorcerie or Witch-craft.

PHI. What I pray you? and how manie are the meanes, whereby the Devill allures persones in anie of these snares?

EPI. Even by these three passiones that are within our selues: Curiositie in great ingines: thrist of revenge, for some tortes deeply apprehended: or greedie appetite of geare, caused through great pouerty. As to the first of these, Curiosity, it is onelie the inticement of Magiciens, or Necromanciers: and the other two are the allureres of the Sorcerers, or Witches, for that olde and craftie Serpent, being a spirite, hee easilie spyes our affections, and so conformes himselfe thereto, to deceaue vs to our wracke.

CHAP. III ARGV.

The significations and Etymologies of the words of Magie and Necromancie. The difference betuixt Necromancie and Witch-craft: What are the entressis, and beginninges, that brings anie to the knowledge thereof.

PHILOMATHES.

I Would gladlie first heare, what thing is it that ye call Magie or Necromancie.

EPI. This worde Magie in the Persian toung, importes as muche as to be ane contemplator or Interpretour of Divine and heavenlie sciences: which being first vsed amongs the Chaldees, through their ignorance of the true divinitie, was esteemed and reputed amongst them, as a principall vertue: And therefore, was named vnjustlie with an honorable stile, which name the Greekes imitated, generally importing all these kindes of vnlawfull artes.

And this word Necromancie is a Greek word, compounded of {Greek Nekrwn} & {Greek manteia}, which is to say, the Prophecie by the dead. This last name is given, to this black & vnlawfull science by the figure Synedoche, because it is a principal part of that art, to serue them selues with dead carcages in their diuinations.

PHI. What difference is there betwixt this arte, and Witch-craft.

EPI. Surelie, the difference vulgare put betwixt them, is verrie merrie, and in a maner true; for they say, that the Witches ar servantes onelie, and slaues to the Devil; but the Necromanciers are his maisters and commanders.

PHI. How can that be true, yt any men being specially adicted to his service, can be his co~manders?

EPI. Yea, they may be: but it is onelie secundum quid: For it is not by anie power that they can haue over him, but ex pacto allanerlie: whereby he oblices himself in some trifles to them, that he may on the other part obteine the fruition of their body & soule. which is the onlie thing he huntes for.

PHI. An verie in-æquitable contract forsooth: But I pray you discourse vnto mee, what is the effect and secreets of that arte?

EPI. That is over large an fielde ye giue mee: yet I shall doe good-will, the most summarlie that I can, to runne through the principal points thereof. As there are two sorts of folkes, that may be entysed to this arte, to wit, learned or vnlearned: so is there two meanes, which are the first steerers vp & feeders of their curiositie, thereby to make them to giue themselves over to the same: Which two meanes, I call the Divels schoole, and his rudimentes. The learned haue their curiositie wakened vppe; and fedde by that which I call his schoole: this is the Astrologie judiciar. For divers men having attained to a great perfection in learning, & yet remaining overbare (alas) of the spirit of regeneration and frutes thereof: finding all naturall thinges common, aswell to the stupide pedants as vnto them, they assaie to vendicate vnto them a greater name. by not onlie knowing the course of things heavenlie, but likewise to clim to the knowledge of things to come thereby. Which, at the first face appearing lawfull vnto them, in respect the ground therof seemeth to proceed of naturall causes onelie: they are so allured thereby, that finding their practize to prooue true in sundry things, they studie to know the cause thereof: and so mounting from degree to degree, vpon the slipperie and vncertaine scale of curiositie; they are at last entised, that where lawfull artes or sciences failes, to satisfie their restles mindes, even to seeke to that black and vnlawfull science of Magie. Where, finding at the first. that such diuers formes of circles & conjurations rightlie joyned thereunto, will raise such divers formes of spirites, to resolue them of their doubts: and attributing the doing thereof, to the power inseparablie tyed, or inherent in the circles: and manie words of God, confusedlie wrapped in; they blindlie glorie of themselves, as if they had by their quicknes of ingine, made a conquest of Plutoes dominion, and were become Emperours over the Stygian habitacles. Where, in the meane time (miserable wretches) they are become in verie deede, bond-slaues to their mortall enemie: and their knowledge, for all that they presume thereof, is nothing increased, except in knowing evill, and the horrors of Hell for punishment thereof, as Adams[1. Gen. 3] was by the eating of the forbidden tree.

CHAP. IIII. ARGV.

The Description of the Rudiments and Schoole, which are the entresses to the arte of Magie: And in speciall the differences betwixt Astronomie and Astrologie: Diuision of Astrologie in diuers partes.

PHILOMATHES.

BVt I pray you likewise forget not to tell what are the Deuilles rudimentes.

EPI. His rudimentes, I call first in generall, all that which is called vulgarly the vertue of worde, herbe, & stone: which is vsed by vnlawful charmes, without naturall causes. As likewise all kinde of practicques, freites, or other like extraordinarie actiones, which cannot abide the true toutche of naturall reason.

PHI. I would haue you to make that playner, by some particular examples; for your proposition is verie generall.

EPI. I meane either by such kinde of Charmes as commonlie dafte wiues vses, for healing of forspoken goodes, for preseruing them from euill eyes, by knitting roun-trees, or sundriest kinde of herbes, to the haire or tailes of the goodes: By curing the Worme, by stemming of blood, by healing of Horse-crookes, by turning of the riddle, or doing of such like innumerable things by wordes, without applying anie thing, meete to the part offended, as Mediciners doe; Or else by staying maried folkes, to haue naturallie adoe with other, (by knitting so manie knottes vpon a poynt at the time of their mariage) And such-like things, which men vses to practise in

their merrinesse: For fra vnlearned men (being naturallie
curious, and lacking the true knowledge of God) findes these
practises to prooue true, as sundrie of them will doe, by the
power of the Devill for deceauing men, and not by anie
inherent vertue in these vaine wordes and freites; & being
desirous to winne a reputation to themselues in such-like
turnes, they either (if they be of the shamefaster sorte) seeke to
bee learned by some that are experimented in that Arte, (not
knowing it to be euill at the first) or else being of the grosser
sorte, runnes directlie to the Deuill for ambition or desire of
gaine, and plainelie contractes with him thereupon.

PHI. But me thinkes these meanes which yee call the Schoole
and rudimentes of the Deuill, are thinges lawfull, and haue
bene approoued for such in all times and ages: As in special,
this science of Astrologie, which is one of the speciall
members of the Mathematicques.

EPI. There are two thinges which the learned haue obserued
from the beginning, in the science of the Heauenlie Creatures,
the Planets, Starres, and such like: The one is their course and
ordinary motiones, which for that cause is called Astronomia:
Which word is a compound of {Greek nomos} & {Greek
asterwn} that is to say, the law of the Starres: And this arte
indeed is one of the members of the Mathematicques, & not
onelie lawful, but most necessarie and commendable. The other
is called Astrologia, being compounded of {Greek asterwn} &
{Greek logos} which is to say, the word, and preaching of the
starres: Which is deuided in two partes: The first by knowing
thereby the powers of simples, and sickenesses, the course of
the seasons and the weather, being ruled by their influence;
which part depending vpon the former, although it be not of it
selfe a parte of Mathematicques: yet it is not vnlawful, being

23

moderatlie vsed, suppose not so necessarie and commendable as the former. The second part is to truste so much to their influences, as thereby to fore-tell what common-weales shall florish or decay: what, persones shall be fortunate or vnfortunate: what side shall winne in anie battell: What man shall obteine victorie at singular combate: What way, and of what age shall men die: What horse shall winne at matche-running; and diuerse such like incredible things, wherein Cardanus, Cornelius Agrippa, and diuerse others haue more curiouslie then profitably written at large. Of this roote last spoken of, springs innumerable branches; such as the knowledge by the natiuities; the Cheiromancie, Geomantie, Hydromantie, Arithmantie, Physiognomie: & a thousand others: which were much practised, & holden in great reuerence by the Gentles of olde. And this last part of Astrologie whereof I haue spoken, which is the root of their branches, was called by them pars fortunæ. This parte now is vtterlie vnlawful to be trusted in, or practized amongst christians, as leaning to no ground of natural reason: & it is this part which I called before the deuils schole.

PHI. But yet manie of the learned are of the contrarie opinion.

EPI. I grant, yet I could giue my reasons to fortifie & maintaine my opinion, if to enter into this disputation it wold not draw me quite off the ground of our discours; besides the mis-spending of the whole daie thereupon: One word onely I will answer to them, & that in the Scriptures (which must be an infallible ground to all true Christians) That in the Prophet Ieremie[1. Ierem. 10] it is plainelie forbidden, to beleeue or hearken vnto them that Prophecies & fore-speakes by the course of the Planets & Starres.

24

CHAP. V. ARGV.

How farre the vsing of Charmes is lawfull or vnlawfull: The
description of the formes of Circkles and Coniurationes. And
what causeth the Magicianes themselues to wearie thereof.

PHILOMATHES.

WELL, Ye haue said far inough in that argument. But how
prooue ye now that these charmes or vnnaturall practicques are
vnlawfull: For so, many honest & merrie men & women haue
publicklie practized some of them, that I thinke if ye would
accuse them al of Witch-craft, ye would affirme more nor ye
will be beleeued in.

EPI. I see if you had taken good tent (to the nature of that
word, whereby I named it,) ye would not haue bene in this
doubt, nor mistaken me, so farre as ye haue done: For although,
as none can be schollers in a schole, & not be subject to the
master thereof: so none can studie and put in practize (for
studie the alone, and knowledge, is more perilous nor
offensiue; and it is the practise only that makes the greatnes of
the offence.) The cirkles and art of Magie, without committing
an horrible defection from God: And yet as they that reades
and learnes their rudiments, are not the more subject to anie
schoole-master, if it please not their parentes to put them to the
schoole thereafter; So they who ignorantly proues these
practicques, which I cal the deuilles rudiments, vnknowing
them to be baites, casten out by him, for trapping such as God
will permit to fall in his hands: This kinde of folkes I saie, no
doubt, ar to be judged the best of, in respect they vse no
invocation nor help of him (by their knowledge at least) in
these turnes, and so haue neuer entred themselues in Sathans

seruice; Yet to speake truely for my owne part (I speake but for my selfe) I desire not to make so neere riding: For in my opinion our enemie is ouer craftie, and we ouer weake (except the greater grace of God) to assay such hazards, wherein he preases to trap vs.

PHI. Ye haue reason forsooth; for as the common Prouerbe saith: They that suppe keile with the Deuill, haue neede of long spoones. But now I praie you goe forwarde in the describing of this arte of Magie.

EPI. Fra they bee come once vnto this perfection in euill, in hauing any knowledge (whether learned or vnlearned) of this black art: they then beginne to be wearie of the raising of their Maister, by conjured circkles; being both so difficile and perilous, and so commeth plainelie to a contract with him, wherein is speciallie conteined formes and effectes.

PHI. But I praye you or euer you goe further, discourse me some-what of their circkles and conjurationes; And what should be the cause of their wearying thereof: For it should seeme that that forme should be lesse fearefull yet, than the direct haunting and societie, with that foule and vncleane Spirite.

EPI. I thinke ye take me to be a Witch my selfe, or at the least would faine sweare your selfe prentise to that craft: Alwaies as I may, I shall shortlie satisfie you, in that kinde of conjurations, which are conteined in such bookes, which I call the Deuilles Schoole: There are foure principall partes; the persons of the conjurers; the action of the conjuration; the wordes and rites vsed to that effect; and the Spirites that are conjured. Ye must first remember to laye the ground, that I tould you before:

which is, that it is no power inherent in the circles, or in the holines of the names of God blasphemouslie vsed: nor in whatsoeuer rites or ceremonies at that time vsed, that either can raise any infernall spirit, or yet limitat him perforce within or without these circles. For it is he onelie, the father of all lyes, who hauing first of all prescribed that forme of doing, feining himselfe to he cornmanded & restreined thereby, wil be loath to passe the boundes of these injunctiones; aswell thereby to make them glory in the impiring ouer him (as I saide before:) As likewise to make himselfe so to be trusted in these little thinges, that he may haue the better commoditie thereafter, to deceiue them in the end with a tricke once for all; I meane the euerlasting perdition of their soul & body. Then laying this ground, as I haue said, these conjurationes must haue few or mo in number of the persones conjurers (alwaies passing the singuler number) according to the qualitie of the circle, and forme of apparition. Two principall thinges cannot well in that errand be wanted: holie-water (whereby the Deuill mockes the Papistes) and some present of a liuing thing vnto him. There ar likewise certaine seasons, dayes and houres, that they obserue in this purpose: These things being all readie, and prepared, circles are made triangular, quadrangular, round, double or single, according to the forme of apparition that they craue. But to speake of the diuerse formes of the circles, of the innumerable characters and crosses that are within and without, and out-through the same, of the diuers formes of apparitiones, that that craftie spirit illudes them with, and of all such particulars in that action, I remit it to ouer-manie that haue busied their heades in describing of the same; as being but curious, and altogether vnprofitable. And this farre onelie I touch, that when the conjured Spirit appeares, which will not be while after manie circumstances, long praiers, and much muttring and murmuring of the conjurers; like a Papist priest, dispatching a hunting Masse: how sone I say, he appeares, if they haue missed one iote of all their rites; or if any of their feete once slyd ouer the circle through terror of his feareful apparition, he payes himselfe at that time in his owne hande, of that due debt which they ought him;, and other-wise would haue delayed longer to haue payed him: I meane hee carries them with him bodie and soule. If this be not now a just cause to make them wearie of these formes of conjuration, I leaue it to you to judge vpon; considering the long-somenesse of the labour, the precise keeping of dayes and houres (as I haue said) The terriblenesse of apparition, and the present perrell that they stande in, in missing the least circumstance or freite, that they ought to obserue: And on the other parte, the Deuil is glad to mooue them to a plaine and square dealing with him as I said before.

CHAP. VI ARGV.

The Deuilles contract with the Magicians: The diuision thereof in two partes: What is the difference betwixt Gods miracles and the Deuils.

PHILOMATHES.

INdeede there is cause inough, but rather to leaue him at all, then to runne more plainlie to him, if they were wise he delt with. But goe forwarde now I pray you to these turnes, fra they become once deacons in this craft.

EPI. From time that they once plainelie begin to contract with him: The effect of their contract consistes in two thinges; in formes and effectes, as I be gan to tell alreadie, were it not yee interrupted me (for although the contract be mutuall; I speake first of that part, wherein the Deuill oblishes himselfe to them) by formes, I meane in what shape or fashion he shall come vnto them, when they call vpon him. And by effectes, I vnderstand, in what special sorts of seruices he bindes himselfe to be subject vnto them. The qualitie of these formes and effectes, is lesse or greater, according to the skil and art of the Magician. For as to the formes, to some of the baser sorte of them he oblishes him selfe to appeare at their calling vpon him, by such a proper name which he shewes vnto them, either in likenes of a dog, a Catte, an Ape, or such-like other beast; or else to answere by a voyce onlie. The effects are to answere to such demands, as concernes curing of disseases, their own particular menagery: or such other base things as they require of him.

But to the most curious sorte, in the formes he will oblish himselfe, to enter in a dead bodie, and there out of to giue such answers, of the euent of battels, of maters concerning the estate of commonwelths, and such like other great questions: yea, to some he will be a continuall attender, in forme of a Page: He will permit himselfe to be conjured, for the space of so many yeres, ether in a tablet or a ring, or such like thing, which they may easely carrie about with them: He giues them power to sel such wares to others, whereof some will bee dearer, and some better cheape; according to the lying or true speaking of the Spirit that is conjured therein. Not but that in verie deede, all Devils must be lyars; but so they abuse the simplicitie of these wretches, that becomes their schollers, that they make them beleeue, that at the fall of Lucifer, some Spirites fell in the aire, some in the fire, some in the water, some in the lande: In which Elementes they still remaine. Whereupon they build, that such as fell in the fire, or in the aire, are truer then they, who fell in the water or in the land, which is al but meare trattles, & forged be the author of al deceit. For they fel not be weight, as a solide substance, to stick in any one parte: But the principall part of their fal, consisting in qualitie, by the falling from the grace of God wherein they were created, they continued still thereafter, and shal do while the latter daie, in wandring through the worlde, as Gods hang-men, to execute such turnes as he employes them in. And when anie of them are not occupyed in that, returne they must to their prison in hel (as it is plaine in the miracle that CHRIST wrought at Gennezareth[1. Mat. 8.]) therein at the latter daie to be all enclosed for euer: and as they deceiue their schollers in this, so do they, in imprinting in them the opinion that there are so manie Princes, Dukes, and Kinges amongst them, euerie one commanding fewer or mo Legions, and impyring in diuers artes, and quarters of the earth. For though that I will not denie that there be a forme of ordour amongst the Angels in Heauen, and consequentlie, was amongst them before their fall; yet, either that they bruike the same sensine; or that God will permit vs to know by damned Deuils, such heauenlie mysteries of his, which he would not reueale to vs neither by Scripture nor Prophets, I thinke no Christiane will once thinke it. But by the contrarie of all such mysteries, as he hath closed vp with his seale of secrecie; it becommeth vs to be contented with an humble ignorance, they being thinges not necessarie for our saluation. But to returne to the purpose, as these formes, wherein Sathan oblishes himselfe to the greatest of the Magicians, are wounderfull curious; so are the effectes correspondent vnto the same: For he will oblish himselfe to teach them artes and sciences, which he may easelie doe, being so learned a knaue as he is: To carrie them newes from anie parte of the worlde, which the agilitie of a Spirite may easelie performe: to reueale to them the secretes of anie persons, so being they bee once spoken, for the thought none knowes but G O D; except so far as yee may ghesse by their countenance, as one who is doubtleslie learned inough in the Physiognomie: Yea, he will make his schollers to creepe in credite with Princes, by fore-telling them manie greate thinges; parte true, parte false: For if all were false, he would tyne credite at all handes; but alwaies doubtsome, as his Oracles were. And he will also make them to please Princes, by faire banquets and daintie dishes, carryed in short space fra the farthest part of the worlde. For no man doubts but he is a thiefe, and his agilitie (as I spake before) makes him to come suche speede. Such-like, he will guard his schollers with faire armies of horse-men and foote-men in appearance, castles and fortes: Which all are but impressiones in the aire, easelie gathered by a spirite, drawing so neare to that substance himselfe: As in like maner he will learne them manie juglarie trickes at Cardes, dice, & such like, to deceiue mennes senses thereby: and such innumerable false practicques; which are prouen by ouer-manie in this age: As they who ar acquainted with that Italian called SCOTO yet liuing, can reporte. And yet are all these thinges but deluding of the senses, and no waies true in substance, as were the false miracles wrought by King Pharaoes Magicians, for counterfeiting Moyses: For that is the difference betuixt Gods myracles and the Deuils, God is a creator, what he makes appeare in miracle, it is so in effect. As Moyses rod being casten downe, was no doubt turned in a natural Serpent: where as the Deuill (as Gods Ape) counterfetting that by his Magicians, maid their wandes to appeare so, onelie to mennes outward senses: as kythed in effect by their being deuoured by the other. For it is no wonder, that the Deuill may delude our senses, since we see by common proofe, that simple juglars will make an hundreth thinges seeme both to our eies and eares otherwaies then they are. Now as to the Magicians parte of the contract, it is in a word that thing, which I said before, the Deuill hunts for in all men.

31

PHI. Surelie ye haue said much to me in this arte, if all that ye haue said be as true as wounderfull.

EPI. For the trueth in these actiones, it will be easelie confirmed, to anie that pleases to take paine vpon the reading of diuerse authenticque histories, and the inquiring of daily experiences. And as for the trueth of their possibilitie, that they may be, and in what maner, I trust I haue alleaged nothing whereunto I haue not joyned such probable reasons, as I leaue to your discretion, to waie and consider: One word onlie I omitted; concerning the forme of making of this contract, which is either written with the Magicians owne bloud: or else being agreed vpon (in termes his schole-master) touches him in some parte, though peraduenture no marke remaine: as it doth with all Witches.

CHAP. VII. ARGV.

The reason why the art of Magie is vnlawfull. What punishment they merite: And who may he accounted guiltie of that crime.

PHILOMATHES.

SVRELIE Ye haue made this arte to appeare verie monstruous & detestable. But what I pray you shall be said to such as mainteines this art to be lawfull, for as euill as you haue made it?

EPI. I say, they sauour of the panne them selues, or at least little better, And yet I would be glad to heare their reasons.

PHI. There are two principallie, that euer I heard vsed; beside
that which is founded vpon the co~mon Prouerb (that the
Necromancers commands the Deuill, which ye haue already
refuted) The one is grounded vpon a receiued custome: The
other vpon an authoritie, which some thinkes infallible. Vpon
custome, we see that diuerse Christian Princes and Magistrates
seuere punishers of Witches, will not onelie ouer-see
Magicians to liue within their dominions; but euen some-times
delight to see them prooue some of their practicques. The other
reason is, that Moyses being brought vp (as it is expreslie said
in the Scriptures) in all the sciences of the AEgyptians;
whereof no doubt, this was one of the principalles. And he
notwithstanding of this arte, pleasing God, as he did,
consequentlie that art professed by so godlie a man, coulde not
be vnlawfull.

EPI. As to the first of your reasones, grounded vpon custome: I
saie, an euill custome can neuer be accepted for a good law, for
the ouer great ignorance of the worde in some Princes and
Magistrates, and the contempt thereof in others, moues them to
sinne heavelie against their office in that poynt. As to the other
reasone, which seemes to be of greater weight, if it were
formed in a Syllogisme; it behooued to be in manie termes, and
full of fallacies (to speake in termes of Logicque) for first, that
that generall proposition; affirming Moyses to be taught in all
the sciences of the AEgyptians, should conclude that he was
taught in Magie, I see no necessity. For we must vnderstand
that the spirit of God there, speaking of sciences, vnderstandes
them that are lawfull; for except they be lawfull, they are but
abusiuè called sciences, & are but ignorances indeede: Nam
homo pictus, non est homo. Secondlie, giuing that he had bene
taught in it, there is great difference, betwixt knowledge and
practising of a thing (as I said before) For God knoweth all

thinges, being alwaies good, and of our sinne & our infirmitie
proceedeth our ignorance. Thirdlie, giuing that he had both
studied and practised the same (which is more nor monstruous
to be beleeued by any Christian) yet we know well inough, that
before that euer the spirite of God began to call Moyses, he
was fled out of AEgypt, being fourtie yeares of age, for the
slaughter of an AEgyptian, and in his good-father Iethroes
lande, first called at the firie bushe, hauing remained there
other fourtie yeares in exile: so that suppose he had beene the
wickeddest man in the worlde before, he then became a
changed and regenerat man, and very litle of olde Moyses
remained in him. Abraham was an Idolater in Vr of Chaldæa,
before he was called: And Paule being called Saule, was a most
sharp persecutor of the Saintes of God, while that name was
changed.

PHI. What punishment then thinke ye merites these Magicians
and Necromancers?

EPI. The like no doubt, that Sorcerers and Witches merites; and
rather so much greater, as their error proceedes of the greater
knowledge, and so drawes nerer to the sin against the holy
Ghost. And as I saye of them, so saye I the like of all such as
consults, enquires, entertaines, & ouersees them, which is
seene by the miserable endes of many that askes councell of
them: For the Deuill hath neuer better tydings to tell to any,
then he tolde to Saule: neither is it lawfull to vse so vnlawfull
instrumentes, were it neuer for so good a purpose: for that
axiome in Theologie is most certaine and infallible: Nunquam
faciendum est malum vt bonum inde eueniat.[1. Ast. 3.]

34

Dæmonologie

The Seconde Booke

CHAP. I. ARGV.

Proued by the Scripture, that such a thing can be: And the reasones refuted of all such as would call it but an imagination and Melancholicque humor.

PHILOMATHES.

NOW Since yee haue satisfied me nowe so fullie, concerning Magie or Necromancie I will pray you to do the like in Sorcerie or Witchcraft.

EPI. That fielde is likewise verie large: and although in the mouthes; and pennes of manie, yet fewe knowes the trueth thereof, so wel as they beleeue themselues, as I shall so shortely as I can, make you (God willing) as easelie to perceiue.

PHI. But I pray you before ye goe further, let mee interrupt you here with a shorte digression: which is, that manie can scarcely beleeue that there is such a thing as Witch-craft. Whose reasons I wil shortely alleage vnto you, that ye may satisfie me as well in that, as ye haue done in the rest. For first, whereas the Scripture seemes to prooue Witchcraft to be, by diuerse examples, and speciallie by sundrie of the same, which ye haue alleaged, it is thought by some, that these places speakes of Magicians and Necromancers onlie, & not of Witches. As in special, these wise men of Pharaohs, that counterfeited Moyses miracles, were Magicians say they, & not Witches: As likewise that Pythonisse that Saul consulted with: And so was Simon Magus in the new Testament, as that very stile importes. Secondlie, where ye would oppone the dailie practicque, & confession of so manie, that is thought likewise to be but verie melancholicque imaginations of simple rauing creatures. Thirdly, if Witches had such power of Witching of folkes to death, (as they say they haue) there had bene none left aliue long sence in the world, but they: at the least, no good or godlie person of whatsoeuer estate, coulde haue escaped their deuilrie.

EPI. Your three reasons as I take, ar grounded the first of them negativè vpon the Scripture: The second affirmativè vpon Physicke: And the thirde vpon the certaine proofe of experience. As to your first, it is most true indeede, that all these wise men of Pharaoh were Magicians of art: As likewise it appeares wel that the Pythonisse, with whom Saul consulted, was of that same profession: & so was Simon Magus. But yee omitted to speake of the Lawe of God, wherein are all Magicians, Diuines, Enchanters, Sorcerers, Witches, & whatsouer of that kinde that consultes with the Deuill, plainelie prohibited, and alike threatned against. And besides that, she who had the Spirite of Python, in the Actes[1. Act. 16.], whose Spirite was put to silence by the Apostle, coulde be no other thing but a verie Sorcerer or Witch. if ye admit the vulgare distinction, to be in a maner true, whereof I spake in the beginning of our conference. For that spirit whereby she conquested such gaine to her Master, was not at her raising or commanding, as she pleased to appoynt, but spake by her toung, aswel publicklie, as priuatelie: Whereby she seemed to

draw nearer to the sort of Demoniakes or possessed, if that
conjunction betwixt them, had not bene of her owne consent:
as it appeared by her, not being tormented therewith: And by
her conquesting of such gaine to her masters (as I haue alreadie
said.) As to your second reason grounded vpon Physick, in
attributing their confessiones or apprehensiones, to a naturall
melancholicque humour: Anie that pleases Physicallie to
consider vpon the naturall humour of melancholie, according to
all the Physicians, that euer writ thereupon, they sall finde that
that will be ouer short a cloak to couer their knauery with: For
as the humor of Melancholic in the selfe is blacke, heauie and
terrene, so are the symptomes thereof, in any persones; that are
subject therevnto, leannes, palenes, desire of solitude: and if
they come to the highest degree therof, mere folie and Manie:
where as by the contrarie, a great nomber of them that euer
haue bene convict or confessors of Witchcraft, as may be
presently scene by manie that haue at this time confessed: they
are by the contrarie, I say, some of them rich and worldly-wise,
some of them fatte or corpulent in their bodies, and most part
of them altogether giuen ouer to the pleasures of the flesh,
continual haunting of companie, and all kind of merrines, both
lawfull and vnlawfull, which are thinges directly contrary to
the symptomes of Melancholie, whereof I spake, and further
experience daylie proues how loath they are to confesse
without torture, which witnesseth their guiltines, where by the
contrary, the Melancholicques neuer spares to bewray
themselues, by their continuall discourses, feeding therby their
humor in that which they thinke no crime. As to your third
reason, it scarselie merites an answere. For if the deuill their
master were not bridled, as the scriptures teacheth vs, suppose
there were no men nor women to be his instrumentes, he could
finde waies inough without anie helpe of others to wrack al
mankinde: wherevnto he employes his whole study, and goeth

about like a roaring Lyon (as PETER saith)[1. 1. Pet. 5] to that effect, but the limites of his power were set down before the foundations of the world were laid, which he hath not power in the least jote to transgresse. But beside all this, there is ouer greate a certainty to proue that they are, by the daily experience of the harmes that they do, both to men, and whatsoeuer thing men possesses, whome God will permit them to be the instrumentes, so to trouble or visite, as in my discourse of that arte, yee shall heare clearelie proued.

CHAP. II ARGV.

The Etymologie and signification of that word of Sorcerie. The first entresse and prentishippe of them that giues themselues to that craft.

PHILOMATHES.

Come on then I pray you, and returne where ye left.

EPI. This word of Sorcerie is a Latine worde, which is taken from casting of the lot, & therefore he that vseth it, is called Sortiarius à sorte. As to the word of Witchcraft, it is nothing but a proper name giuen in our language. The cause wherefore they were called sortiarij, proceeded of their practicques seeming to come of lot or chance: Such as the turning of the riddle: the knowing of the forme of prayers, or such like tokens: If a person diseased woulde liue or dye. And in generall, that name was giuen them for vsing of such charmes, and freites, as that Crafte teacheth them. Manie poynts of their craft and practicques are common betuixt the Magicians and them: for they serue both one Master, althought in diuerse fashions. And as I deuided the Necromancers, into two sorts,

learned and vnlearned; so must I denie them in other two, riche
and of better accompt, poore and of basser degree. These two
degrees now of persones, that practises this craft, answers to
the passions in them, which (I told you before) the Deuil vsed
as meanes to intyse them to his seruice, for such of them as are
in great miserie and pouertie, he allures to follow him, by
promising vnto them greate riches, and worldlie commoditie.
Such as though riche, yet burnes in a desperat desire of
reuenge, hee allures them by promises, to get their turne
satisfied to their hartes contentment. It is to be noted nowe, that
that olde and craftie enemie of ours, assailes none, though
touched with any of these two extremities, except he first finde
an entresse reddy for him, either by the great ignorance of the
person he deales with, ioyned with an euill life, or else by their
carelesnes and contempt of God: And finding them in an vtter
despair, for one of these two former causes that I haue spoken
of; he prepares the way by feeding them craftely in their
humour, and filling them further and further with despaire,
while he finde the time proper to discouer himself vnto them.
At which time, either vpon their walking solitarie in the fieldes,
or else lying pansing in their bed; but alwaies without the
company of any other, he either by a voyce, or in likenesse of a
man inquires of them, what troubles them: and promiseth them,
a suddaine and certaine waie of remedie, vpon condition on the
other parte, that they follow his advise; and do such thinges as
he wil require of them: Their mindes being prepared before
hand, as I haue alreadie spoken, they easelie agreed vnto that
demande of his: And syne settes an other tryist, where they
may meete againe. At which time, before he proceede any
further with them, he first perswades them to addict themselues
to his seruice: which being easely obteined, he then discouers
what he is vnto them: makes them to renunce their God and
Baptisme directlie, and giues them his marke vpon some secreit

place of their bodie, which remaines soare vnhealed, while his next meeting with them, and thereafter euer insensible, how soeuer it be nipped or pricked by any, as is dailie proued, to giue them a proofe thereby, that as in that doing, hee could hurte and heale them; so all their ill and well doing thereafter, must depende vpon him. And besides that, the intollerable dolour that they feele in that place, where he hath marked them, serues to waken them, and not to let them rest, while their next meeting againe: fearing least otherwaies they might either forget him, being as new Prentises, and not well inough founded yet, in that fiendlie follie: or else remembring of that horrible promise they made him, at their last meeting, they might skunner at the same, and preasse to call it back. At their thirde meeting, he makes a shew to be carefull, to performe his promises, either by teaching them waies howe to get themselues reuenged, if they be of that sort: Or els by teaching them lessons, how by moste vilde and vnlawfull meanes, they may obtaine gaine, and worldlie commoditie, if they be of the other sorte.

CHAP. III. ARGV.

The Witches actiones diuided in two partes. The actiones proper to their owne persones. Their actiones toward others. The forme of their conuentiones, and adoring of their Master.

PHILOMATHES.

YE haue said now inough of their initiating in that ordour. It restes then that ye discourse vpon their practises, fra they be passed Prentises: for I would faine heare what is possible to them to performe in verie deede. Although they serue a common Master with the Necromancers, (as I haue before

saide) yet serue they him in an other forme. For as the meanes
are diuerse, which allures them to these vnlawfull artes of
seruing of the Deuill; so by diuerse waies vse they their
practises, answering to these meanes, which first the Deuill,
vsed as instrumentes in them; though al tending to one end: To
wit. the enlargeing of Sathans tyrannie, and crossing of the
propagation of the Kingdome of CHRIST, so farre as lyeth in
the possibilitie, either of the one or other sorte, or of the Deuill
their Master. For where the Magicians, as allured by curiositie,
in the most parte of their practises, seekes principallie the
satisfying of the same, and to winne to themselues a popular
honoure and estimation:

These Witches on the other parte, being intised ether for the
desire of reuenge, or of worldly riches, their whole practises
are either to hurte men and their gudes, or what they possesse,
for satisfying of their cruell mindes in the former, or else by the
wracke in quhatsoeuer sorte, of anie whome God will permitte
them to haue power off, to satisfie their greedie desire in the
last poynt.

EPI. In two partes their actiones may be diuided; the actiones
of their owne persones, and the actiones proceeding from them
towardes anie other. And this diuision being wel vnderstood,
will easilie resolue you, what is possible to them to doe. For
although all that they confesse is no lie vpon their parte, yet
doubtlesly in my opinion, a part of it is not indeede, according
as they take it to be: And in this I meane by the actiones of
their owne persones. For as I said before, speaking of Magie
that the Deuill illudes the senses of these schollers of his, in
manie thinges, so saye I the like of these Witches.

PHI. Then I pray you, first to speake of that part of their owne persons, and syne ye may come next to their actiones towardes; others.

EPI. To the effect that they may performe such seruices of their false Master, as he employes them in, the deuill as Gods Ape, counterfeites in his seruantes this seruice & forme of adoration, that God prescribed and made his seruantes to practise. For as the seruants of G O D, publicklie vses to conveene for seruing of him, so makes he them in great numbers to conveene (though publickly they dare not) for his seruice. As none conueenes to the adoration and worshipping of God, except they be marked with his seale, the Sacrament of Baptisme: So none serues Sathan, and conueenes to the adoring of him, that are not marked with that marke, wherof I alredy spake. As the Minister sent by God, teacheth plainely at the time of their publick conuentions, how to serue him in spirit & truth: so that vncleane spirite, in his owne person teacheth his Disciples, at the time of their conueening, how to worke all kinde of mischiefe: And craues compt of all their horrible and detestable proceedinges passed, for aduancement of his seruice. Yea, that he may the more viuelie counterfeit and scorne God, he oft times makes his slaues to conveene in these verrie places, which are destinat and ordeined for the conveening of the servantes of God (I meane by Churches) But this farre, which I haue yet said, I not onelie take it to be true in their opiniones, but euen so to be indeede. For the forme that he vsed in counterfeiting God amongst the Gentiles, makes me so to thinke: As God spake by his Oracles, spake he not so by his? As G O D had aswell bloudie Sacrifices, as others without bloud, had not he the like? As God had Churches sanctified to his seruice, with Altars, Priests, Sacrifices, Ceremonies and Prayers; had he not the like polluted to his seruice? As God

gaue responses by Vrim and Thummim, gaue he not his
responses by the intralls of beastes, by the singing of Fowles,
and by their actiones in the aire? As God by visiones, dreames,
and extases reueiled what was to come, and what was his will
vnto his scruantes; vsed he not the like meanes to forwarne his
slaues of things to come? Yea, euen as God loued cleannes,
hated vice, and impuritie, & appoynted punishmentes
therefore: vsed he not the like (though falselie I grant, and but
in eschewing the lesse inconuenient, to draw them upon a
greater) yet dissimuled he not I say, so farre as to appoynt his
Priestes to keepe their bodies cleane and vndefiled, before their
asking responses of him? And feyned he not God to be a
protectour of euerie vertue, and a iust reuenger of the
contrarie? This reason then moues me. that as he is that same
Deuill; and as craftie nowe as he was then; so wil hee not spare
a pertelie in these actiones that I haue spoken of, concerning
the witches persones: But further, Witches oft times confesses
not only his conueening in the Church with them, but his
occupying of the Pulpit: Yea, their forme of adoration, to be
the kissing of his hinder partes. Which though it seeme
ridiculous, yet may it likewise be true, seeing we reade that in
Calicute, he appearing in forme of a Goate-bucke, hath
publicklie that vn-honest homage done vnto him, by euerie one
of the people: So ambitious is he, and greedie of honour (which
procured his fall) that he will euen imitate God in that parte,
where it is said, that Moyses could see but the hinder partes of
God, for the brightnesse of his glorie:[1. Exo. 33] And yet that
speache is spoken but {Greek anðrwpwpaðeian}

CHAP. IIII. ARGV.

What are the waies possible, wherby the witches may transport themselues to places far distant. And what ar impossible &mere illusiones of Sathan. And the reasons therof.

PHILOMATHES.

Bvt by what way say they or think ye it possible that they can com to these vnlawful co~uentio~s?

EPI. There is the thing which I esteeme their senses to be deluded in, and though they lye not in confessing of it, because they thinke it to be true, yet not to be so in substance or effect: for they saie, that by diuerse meanes they may conueene, either to the adoring of their Master, or to the putting in practise any seruice of his, committed vnto their charge: one way is natural, which is natural riding, going or sayling, at what houre their Master comes and aduertises them. And this way may be easelie beleued: an other way is some-what more strange: and yet is it possible to be true: which is by being carryed by the force of the Spirite which is their conducter, either aboue the earth or aboue the Sea swiftlie, to the place where they are to meet: which I am perswaded to be likewaies possible, in respect that as Habakkuk was carryed by the Angell in that forme, to the denne where Daniell laie;[1. Apocrypha of Bell and the Dragon.] so thinke I, the Deuill will be reddie to imitate God, as well in that as in other thinges: which is much more possible to him to doe, being a Spirite, then to a mighty winde, being but a naturall meteore, to transporte from one place to an other a solide bodie, as is commonlie and dailie seene in practise: But in this violent forme they cannot be carryed, but a shorte boundes, agreeing with the space that they may reteine their breath: for if it were longer, their breath could not remaine vnextinguished, their bodie being carryed in such a violent & forceable maner, as be example: If one fall off an small height, his life is but in perrell, according to the harde or soft lighting: But if one fall from an high and stay rocke, his breath wilbe forceablie banished from the bodie, before he can win to the earth, as is oft seen by experience. And in this transporting they say themselues, that they are inuisible to anie other, except amongst themselues; which may also be possible in my opinion. For if the deuil may forme what kinde of impressiones he pleases in the aire, as I haue said before, speaking of Magie, why may he not far easilier thicken & obscure so the air, that is next about them by contracting it strait together, that the beames of any other mans eyes, cannot pearce thorow the same, to see them? But the third way of their comming to their conuentions, is, that where in I think them deluded: for some of them sayeth, that being transformed in the likenesse of a little beast or foule, they will come and pearce through whatsoeuer house or Church, though all ordinarie passages be closed, by whatsoeuer open, the aire may enter in at. And some sayeth, that their bodies lying stil as in an extasy, their spirits wil be rauished out of their bodies, & caried to such places. And for verefying therof, wil giue euident tokens, aswel by witnesses that haue seene their body lying senseles in the meane time, as by naming persones, whomwith they mette, and giuing tokens quhat purpose was amongst them, whome otherwaies they could not haue knowen: for this forme of journeing, they affirme to vse most, when they are transported from one Countrie to another.

PHI. Surelie I long to heare your owne opinion of this: For they are like old wiues trattles about the fire. The reasons that moues me to thinke that these are meere illusiones, ar these.

First for them that are transformed in likenes of beastes or foules, can enter through so narrow passages, although I may easelie beleeue that the Deuill coulde by his woorkemanshippe vpon the aire, make them appeare to be in such formes, either to themselues or to others: Yet how he can contract a solide bodie within so little roome, I thinke it is directlie contrarie to it selfe, for to be made so little, and yet not diminished: To be so straitlie drawen together, and yet feele no paine; I thinke it is so contrarie to the qualitie of a naturall bodie, and so like to the little transubstantiat god in the Papistes Masse, that I can neuer beleeue it. So to haue a quantitie, is so proper to a solide bodie, that as all Philosophers concludes, it cannot be any more without one, then a spirite can haue one. For when PETER came out of the prison, and the doores all locked:[1. Act. 12.] It was not by any contracting of his bodie in so little roome: but by the giuing place of the dore, though vn-espyed by the Gaylors. And yet is there no comparison, when this is done, betuixt the power of God, and of the Deuill. As to their forme of extasie and spirituall transporting, it is certaine the soules going out of the bodie, is the onely difinition of naturall death: and who are once dead, God forbid wee should thinke that it should lie in the power of all the Deuils in Hell, to restore them to their life againe: Although he can put his owne spirite in a dead bodie, which the Necromancers commonlie practise, as yee haue harde. For that is the office properly belonging to God; and besides that, the soule once parting from the bodie, cannot wander anie longer in the worlde, but to the owne resting place must it goe immediatlie, abiding the conjunction of the bodie againe, at the latter daie. And what CHRIST or the Prophets did miraculouslie in this case, it cannot in no Christian mans opinion be maid common with the Deuill. As for anie tokens that they giue for proouing of this, it is verie possible to the Deuils craft, to perswade them to these meanes.

For he being a spirite, may hee: not so rauishe their thoughtes, and dull their sences, that their bodie lying as dead, hee may object to their spirites as it were in a dreame, & (as the Poets write of Morpheus) represente such formes of persones, of places, and other circumstances, as he pleases to illude them with? Yea, that he maie deceiue them with the greater efficacie, may hee not at that same instant, by fellow angelles of his, illude such other persones so in that same fashion, whome with he makes them to beleeue that they mette; that all their reportes and tokens, though seuerallie examined, may euerie one agree with an other. And that whatsoeuer actiones, either in hurting men or beasts: or whatsoeuer other thing that they falselie imagine, at that time to haue done, may by himselfe or his marrowes, at that same time be done indeede; so as if they would giue for a token of their being rauished at the death of such a person within so shorte space thereafter, whom they beleeue to haue poysoned, or witched at that instante, might hee not at that same houre, haue smitten that same person by the permission of G O D, to the farther deceiuing of them, and to mooue others to beleeue them? And this is surelie the likeliest way, and most according to reason, which my judgement can finde out in this, and whatsoeuer vther vnnaturall poyntes of their confession. And by these meanes shall we saill surelie, betuixt Charybdis and Scylla, in eschewing the not beleeuing of them altogether on the one part, least that drawe vs to the errour that there is no Witches: and on the other parte in beleeuing of it, make vs to eschew the falling into innumerable absurdities, both monstruouslie against all Theologie diuine, and Philosophie humaine.

CHAP. V ARGV.

Witches actiones towardes others. Why there are more women of that craft nor men? What thinges are possible to them to effectuate by the power of their master. The reasons thereof. What is the surest remedie of the harmes done by them.

PHILOMATHES.

Forsooth your opinion in this, seemes to carrie most reason with it, and sence yee haue ended, then the actions belonging properly to their owne persones: say forwarde now to their actiones vsed towardes others.

EPI. In their actiones vsed towardes others, three thinges ought to be considered: First the maner of their consulting thereupon: Next their part as instrumentes: And last their masters parte, who puts the same in execution. As to their consultationes thereupon, they vse them oftest in the Churches, where they conveene for adoring: at what time their master enquiring at them what they would be at: euerie one of them propones vnto him, what wicked turne they would haue done, either for obteining of riches, or for reuenging them vpon anie whome they haue malice at: who granting their demande, as no doubt willinglie he wil, since it is to doe euill, he teacheth them the means, wherby they may do the same. As for little trifling turnes that women haue ado with, he causeth them to ioynt dead corpses, & to make powders thereof, mixing such other thinges there amongst, as he giues vnto them.

PHI. But before yee goe further, permit mee I pray you to interrupt you one worde, which yee haue put mee in memorie of, by speaking of Women. What can be the cause that there are twentie women giuen to that craft, where ther is one man?

EPI. The reason is easie, for as that sexe is frailer then man is, so is it easier to be intrapped in these grosse snares of the Deuill, as was ouer well proued to be true, by the Serpents deceiuing of Eua at the beginning, which makes him the homelier with that sexe sensine.

PHI. Returne now where ye left.

EPI. To some others at these times hee teacheth, how to make Pictures of waxe or clay: That by the rosting thereof, the persones; that they beare the name of, may be continuallie melted or dryed awaie by continuall sicknesse. To some hee giues such stones or poulders, as will helpe to cure or cast on diseases: And to some he teacheth kindes of vncouthe poysons, which Mediciners vnderstandes not (for he is farre cunningner then man in the knowledge of all the occult proprieties of nature) not that anie of these meanes which hee teacheth them (except the poysons which are composed of thinges naturall) can of them selues helpe any thing to these turnes, that they are employed in, but onelie being Gods Ape, as well in that, as in all other thinges. Even as God by his Sacramentes which are earthlie of themselues workes a heauenlie effect, though no waies by any cooperation in them: And as CHRIST by clay & spettle wrought together, opened the eies of the blynd man,[1. John. 9.] suppose there was no vertue in that which he outwardlie applyed, so the Deuill will haue his out-warde meanes to be shewes as it were of his doing, which hath no part of cooperation in his turnes with him, how farre that euer the ignorantes be abused in the contrarie. And as to the effectes of these two former partes, to wit, the consultationes and the outward meanes, they are so wounderfull as I dare not allege anie of them, without ioyning a sufficient reason of the possibilitie thereof. For leauing all the small trifles among

49

wiues, and to speake of the principall poyntes of their craft. For
the common trifles thereof, they can do without conuerting
well inough by themselues: These principall poyntes I say are
these: They can make men or women to loue or hate other,
which may be verie possible to the Deuil to effectuat, seing he
being a subtile spirite, knowes well inough how to perswade
the corrupted affection of them whom God will permit him so
to deale with: They can lay the siknesse of one vpon an other,
which likewise is verie possible vnto him: For since by Gods
permission, he layed siknesse vpon IOB, why may he not farre
easilier lay it vpon any other: For as an old practisian, he
knowes well inough what humor domines most in anie of vs,
and as a spirite hee can subtillie walken vp the same, making it
peccant, or to abounde, as he thinkes meete for troubling of vs,
when God will so permit him. And for the taking off of it, no
doubt he will be glad to reliue such of present paine, as he may
thinke by these meanes to perswade to bee catched in his
euerlasting snares and fetters. They can be-witch and take the
life of men or women, by rosting of the Pictures, as I spake of
before, which likewise is verie possible to their Master to
performe, for although, (as I saide before) that instrumente of
waxe haue no vertue in that turne doing, yet may hee not verie
well euen by that same measure that his conjured slaues meltes
that waxe at the fire, may he not I say at these same times,
subtilie as a spirite so weaken and scatter the spirites of life of
the patient, as may make him on th'one part, for faintnesse to
sweate out the humour of his bodie: And on the other parte, for
the not concurrence of these spirites, which causes his
digestion, so debilitat his stomak, that his humour radicall
continually, sweating out on the one parte, and no new good
suck being put in the place thereof, for lack of digestion on the
other, hee at last shall vanish awaie, euen as his picture will
doe at the fire. And that knauish and cunning woorkeman, by

50

troubling him onely at some times, makes a proportion so neare betuixt the woorking of the one and the other, that both shall ende as it were at one time. They can rayse stormes and tempestes in the aire, either vpon Sea or land, though not vniuersally, but in such a particular place and prescribed boundes, as God will permitte them so to trouble: Which likewise is verie easie to be discerned from anie other naturall tempestes that are meteores, in respect of the suddaine and violent raising thereof, together with the short induring of the same. And this is likewise verie possible to their master to do, he hauing such affinitie with the aire as being a spirite, and hauing such power of the forming and moouing thereof, as ye haue heard me alreadie declare: For in the Scripture, that stile of the Prince of the aire is giuen vnto him[1. Ephes. 2]. They can make folkes to becom phrenticque or Maniacque, which likewise is very possible to their master to do, sence they are but naturall sicknesses: and so he may lay on these kindes, aswell as anie others. They can make spirites either to follow and trouble persones, or haunt certaine houses. and affraie oftentimes the inhabitantes: as hath bene knowen to be done by our Witches at this time. And likewise they can make some to be possessed with spirites, & so to becom verie Dæmoniacques: and this last sorte is verie possible likewise to the Deuill their Master to do, since he may easilie send his owne angells to trouble in what forme he pleases, any whom God wil permit him so to vse.

PHI. But will God permit these wicked instrumentes by the power of the Deuill their master, to trouble by anie of these meanes, anie that beleeues in him?

EPI. No doubt, for there are three kinde of folkes whom God will permit so to be tempted or troubled; the wicked for their

horrible sinnes, to punish them in the like measure; The godlie
that are sleeping in anie great sinnes or infirmities and
weakenesse in faith, to waken them vp the faster by such an
vncouth forme: and euen some of the best, that their patience
may bee tryed before the world, as IOBs was. For why may not
God vse anie kinde of extraordinarie punishment, when it
pleases him; as well as the ordinarie roddes of sicknesse or
other aduersities.

PHI. Who then may he free from these Deuilish practises?

EPI. No man ought to presume so far as to promise anie
impunitie to himselfe: for God hath before all beginninges
preordinated aswell the particular sortes of Plagues as of
benefites for euerie man, which in the owne time he ordaines
them to be visited with, & yet ought we not to be the more
affrayde for that, of any thing that the Deuill and his wicked
instrumentes can do against vs.. For we dailie fight against the
Deuill in a hundreth other waies: And therefore as a valiant
Captaine, affraies no more being at the combat, nor stayes from
his purpose for the rummishing shot of a Cannon, nor the small
clack of a Pistoler: suppose he be not certaine what may light
vpon him; Euen so ought we boldlie to goe forwarde in
fighting against the Deuill without anie greater terrour, for
these his rarest weapons, nor for the ordinarie whereof wee
haue daily the proofe.

PHI. Is it not lawfull then by the helpe of some other Witche to
cure the disease that is casten on by that craft?

EPI. No waies lawfull: For I gaue you the reason thereof in that
axiome of Theologie, which was the last wordes I spake of
Magie

PHI. How then may these diseases he lawfullie cured?

EPI. Onelie by earnest prayer to G O D, by amendement of their liues, and by sharp persewing euerie one, according to his calling of these instrumentes of Sathan, whose punishment to the death will be a salutarie sacrifice for the patient. And this is not onely the lawfull way, but likewise the most sure: For by the Deuils meanes, can neuer the Deuill be casten out,[1. Math. 3] as Christ sayeth. And when such a cure is vsed, it may wel serue for a shorte time, but at the Last, it will doubtleslie tend to the vtter perdition of the patient, both in bodie and soule.

CHAP. VI. ARGV.

What sorte of folkes are least or most subiect to receiue harme by Witchcraft. What power they haue to harme the Magistrate, and vpon what respectes they haue any power in prison: And to what end may or will the Deuill appeare to them therein. Vpon what respectes the Deuill appeires in sundry shapes to sundry of them at any time.

PHILOMATHES.

BVt who dare take vpon him to punish them, if no man can be sure to be free from their vnnaturall inuasiones?

EPI. We ought not the more of that restraine from vertue, that the way wherby we climbe thereunto be straight and perrilous. But besides that, as there is no kinde of persones so subject to receiue harme of them, as these that are of infirme and weake faith (which is the best buckler against such inuasiones:) so haue they so smal power ouer none) as ouer such as zealouslie and earnestlie persewes them, without sparing for anie worldlie respect.

PHI. Then they are like the Pest, which smites these sickarest, that flies it farthest, and apprehends deepliest the perrell thereof.

EPI. It is euen so with them: For neither is it able to them to vse anie false cure vpon a patient, except the patient first beleeue in their power, and so hazard the tinsell of his owne soule, nor yet can they haue lesse power to hurte anie, nor such as contemnes most their doinges, so being it comes of faith, and not of anie vaine arrogancie in themselues.

PHI. But what is their power against the Magistrate?

EPI. Lesse or greater, according as he deales with them. For if he be slouthfull towardes them, God is verie able to make them instrumentes to waken & punish his slouth. But if he be the contrarie, he according to the iust law of God, and allowable law of all Nationes, will be diligent in examining and punishing of them: G O D will not permit their master to trouble or hinder so good a woorke.

PHI. But fra they be once in handes and firmance, haue they anie further power in their craft?

EPI. That is according to the forme of their detention. If they be but apprehended and deteined by anie priuate person, vpon other priuate respectes, their power no doubt either in escaping, or in doing hurte, is no lesse nor euer it was before. But if on the other parte, their apprehending and detention be by the lawfull Magistrate, vpon the iust respectes of their guiltinesse in that craft, their power is then no greater then before that euer they medled with their master. For where God beginnes iustlie to strike by his lawfull Lieutennentes, it is not in the Deuilles power to defraude or bereaue him of the office, or effect of his powerfull and reuenging Scepter.

PHI. But will neuer their master come to visite them, fra they be once apprehended and put in firmance?

EPI. That is according to the estaite that these miserable wretches are in: For if they be obstinate in still denying, he will not spare, when he findes time to speake with them, either if he finde them in anie comfort, to fill them more and more with the vaine hope of some maner of reliefe: or else if hee finde them in a deepe dispaire, by all meanes to augment the same, and to perswade them by some extraordinarie meanes to put themselues downe, which verie commonlie they doe. But if they be penitent and confesse, God will not permit him to trouble them anie more with his presence and alurementes.

PHI It is not good vsing his counsell I see then. But I woulde earnestlie know when he appeares to them in Prison, what formes vses he then to take?

EPI. Diuers formes, euen as he vses to do at other times vnto them. For as I told you, speking of Magie, lie appeares to that kinde of craftes-men ordinarily in an forme, according as they agree vpon it amongst themselues: Or if they be but prentises, according to the qualitie of their circles or conjuratiures: Yet to these capped creatures, he appeares as he pleases, and as he findes meetest for their humors. For euen at their publick conuentiones, he appeares to diuers of them in diuers formes, as we haue found by the difference of their confessiones in that point: For he deluding them with vaine impressiones in the aire, makes himselfe to seeme more terrible to the grosser sorte, that they maie thereby be moued to feare and reuerence him the more: And les monstrous and vncouthlike againe to the craftier sorte, least otherwaies they might sturre and skunner at his vglinesse.

PHI. How can he then be felt. as they confesse they haue done him, if his bodie be but of aire?

EPI. I heare little of that amongst their confessiones, yet may he make himselfe palpable, either by assuming any dead bodie, and vsing the ministrie thereof, or else by deluding as wel their sence of feeling as seeing; which is not impossible to him to doe, since all our senses, as we are so weake, and euen by ordinarie sicknesses will be often times deluded.

PHI. But I would speere one worde further yet, concerning his appearing to them in prison, which is this. May any other that chances to be present at that time in the prison, see him as well as they.

EPI. Some-times they will, and some-times not, as it pleases God.

CHAP. VII. ARGV.

Two formes of the deuils visible conuersing in the earth, with the reasones wherefore the one of them was communest in the time of Papistrie: And the other sensine. Those that denies the power of the Deuill, denies the power of God, and are guiltie of the errour of the Sadduces.

PHILOMATHES.

HAth the Deuill then power to appeare to any other, except to such as are his sworne disciples: especially since al Oracles, & such like kinds of illusiones were taken awaie and abolished by the cumming Of CHRIST?

EPI. Although it be true indeede, that the brightnesse of the Gospell at his cumming, scaled the cloudes of all these grosse errors in the Gentilisme: yet that these abusing spirites, ceases not sensine at sometimes to appeare, dailie experience teaches vs. Indeede this difference is to be marked betwixt the formes of Sathans conuersing visiblie in the world. For of two different formes thereof, the one of them by the spreading of the Euangell, and conquest of the white horse, in the sixt Chapter of the Reuelation, is much hindred and become rarer there through. This his appearing to any Christians, troubling of them outwardly, or possessing of them constraynedly. The other of them is become communer and more vsed sensine, I meane by their vnlawfull artes, whereupon our whole purpose hath bene. This we finde by experience in this Ile to be true. For as we know, moe Ghostes and spirites were seene, nor tongue can tell, in the time of blinde Papistrie in these Countries, where now by the contrarie, a man shall scarcely all his time here once of such things. And yet were these vnlawfull artes farre rarer at that time: and neuer were so much harde of, nor so rife as they are now.

PHI. What should be the cause of that?

EPI. The diuerse nature of our sinnes procures at the Iustice of God, diuerse sortes of punishments answering thereunto. And therefore as in the time of Papistrie, our fathers erring grosselie, & through ignorance, that mist of errours ouershaddowed the Deuill to walke the more familiarlie amongst them: And as it were by barnelie and affraying terroures, to mocke and accuse their barnelie erroures. By the contrarie, we now being sounde of Religion, and in our life rebelling to our profession, God iustlie by that sinne of rebellion, as Samuel calleth it, accuseth our life so wilfullie fighting against our profession.

PHI. Since yee are entred now to speake of the appearing of spirites: I would be glad to heare your opinion in that matter. For manie denies that anie such spirites can appeare in these daies as I haue said.

EPI. Doubtleslie who denyeth the power of the Deuill, woulde likewise denie the power of God, if they could for shame. For since the Deuill is the verie contrarie opposite to God, there can be no better way to know God, then by the contrarie; as by the ones power (though a creature) to admire the power of the great Creator: by the falshood of the one to considder the trueth of the other, by the injustice of the one, to considder the Iustice of the other: And by the cruelty of the one, to considder the mercifulnesse of the other: And so foorth in all the rest of the essence of God, and qualities of the Deuill. But I feare indeede, there be ouer many Sadduces in this worlde, that denies all kindes of spirites: For convicting of whose errour, there is cause inough if there were no more, that God should permit at sometimes spirits visiblie to kyith.

Dæmonologie

The Thirde Booke

CHAP. I. ARGV.

The diuision of spirites in foure principall kindes. The description of the first kinde of them, called Spectra & vmbræ mortuorum. What is the best way to be free of their trouble.

PHILOMATHES.

I Pray you now then go forward in telling what ye thinke fabulous, or may be trowed in that case.

EPI. That kinde of the Deuils conuersing in the earth, may be diuided in foure different kindes, whereby he affrayeth and troubleth the bodies of men: For of the abusing of the soule, I haue spoken alreadie. The first is, where spirites troubles some houses or solitarie places: The second, where spirites followes vpon certaine persones, and at diuers houres troubles them: The thirde, when they enter within them and possesse them: The fourth is these kinde of spirites that are called vulgarlie the Fayrie. Of the three former kindes, ye harde alreadie, how they may artificiallie be made by Witch-craft to trouble folke: Now it restes to speake of their naturall comming as it were, and not raysed by Witch-craft. But generally I must for-warne you of one thing before I enter in this purpose: that is, that although in my discourseing of them, I deuyde them in diuers kindes, yee

59

must notwithstanding there of note my Phrase of speaking in
that: For doubtleslie they are in effect, but all one kinde of
spirites, who for abusing the more of mankinde. takes on these
sundrie shapes, and vses diuerse formes of out-ward actiones,
as if some were of nature better then other. Nowe I returne to
my purpose: As to the first kinde of these spirites, that were
called by the auncients by diuers names, according as their
actions were. For if they were spirites that haunted some
houses, by appearing in diuers and horrible formes, and making
greate dinne: they were called Lemures or Spectra. If they
appeared in likenesse of anie defunct to some friends of his,
they wer called vmbræ mortuorum: And so innumerable stiles
they got, according to their actiones, as I haue said alreadie. As
we see by experience, how manie stiles they haue given them
in our language in the like maner: Of the appearing of these
spirites, wee are certified by the Scriptures, where the Prophet
ESAY 13. and 34. cap. threatning the destruction of Babell and
Edom:[1. Esay. 13 Iere. 50] declares, that it shal not onlie be
wracked, but shall become so greate a solitude, as it shall be
the habitackle of Howlettes, and of ZIIM and IIM, which are
the proper Hebrewe names for these Spirites. The cause whie
they haunte solitarie places, it is by reason, that they may
affraie and brangle the more the faith of suche as them alone
hauntes such places. For our nature is such, as in companies
wee are not so soone mooued to anie such kinde of feare, as
being solitare, which the Deuill knowing well inough, hee will
not therefore assaile vs but when we are weake: And besides
that, G O D will not permit him so to dishonour the societies
and companies of Christians, as in publicke times and places to
walke visiblie amongst them. On the other parte, when he
troubles certaine houses that are dwelt in, it is a sure token
either of grosse ignorance, or of some grosse and slanderous

sinnes amongst the inhabitantes thereof: which God by that extraordinarie rod punishes.

PHI. But by what way or passage can these Spirites enter in these houses, seeing they alledge that they will enter, Doore and Window being steiked?

EPI. They will choose the passage for their entresse, according to the forme that they are in at that time. For if they haue assumed a deade bodie, whereinto they lodge themselues, they can easely inough open without dinne anie Doore or Window, and enter in thereat. And if they enter as a spirite onelie, anie place where the aire may come in at, is large inough an entrie for them: For as I said before, a spirite can occupie no quantitie.

PHI. And will God then permit these wicked spirites to trouble the reste of a dead bodie, before the resurrection thereof? Or if he will so, I thinke it should be of the reprobate onely.

EPI. What more is the reste troubled of a dead bodie, when the Deuill carryes it out of the Graue to serue his turne for a space, nor when the Witches takes it vp and joyntes it, or when as Swine wortes vppe the graues? The rest of them that the Scripture speakes of, is not meaned by a locall remaining continuallie in one place, but by their resting from their trauelles and miseries of this worlde, while their latter conjunction againe with the soule at that time to receaue full glorie in both. And that the Deuill may vse aswell the ministrie of the bodies of the faithfull in these cases, as of the vn-faithfull, there is no inconvenient; for his haunting with their bodies after they are deade, can no-waies defyle them: In respect of the soules absence. And for anie dishonour it can be vnto them, by what reason can it be greater, then the hanging, heading, or many such shameful deaths, that good men will suffer? for there is nothing in the bodies of the faithfull, more worthie of honour, or freer from corruption by nature, nor in these of the vnfaithful, while time they be purged and glorified in the latter daie, as is dailie seene by the vilde diseases and corruptions, that the bodies of the faythfull are subject vnto, as yee will see clearelie proued, when I speake of the possessed and Dæmoniacques.

PHI. Yet there are sundrie that affirmes to haue haunted such places, where these spirites are alleaged to be: And coulde neuer heare nor see anie thing.

EPI. I thinke well: For that is onelie reserued to the secreete knowledge of God, whom he wil permit to see such thinges, and whome not.

PHI. But where these spirites hauntes and troubles anie houses, what is the best waie to banishe them?

EPI. By two meanes may onelie the remeid of such things be procured: The one is ardent prayer to God, both of these persones that are troubled with them, and of that Church whereof they are. The other is the purging of themselues by amende ment of life from such sinnes. as haue procured that extraordinarie plague.

PHI. And what meanes then these kindes of spirites, when they appeare in the shaddow of a person newlie dead, or to die, to his friendes?

EPI. When they appeare vpon that occasion, they are called Wraithes in our language. Amongst the Gentiles the Deuill vsed that much, to make them beleeue that it was some good spirite that appeared to them then, ether to forewarne them of the death of their friend; or else to discouer vnto them, the will of the defunct, or what was the way of his slauchter, as is written in the booke of the histories Prodigious. And this way hee easelie decciued the Gentiles, because they knew not God: And to that same effect is it, that he now appeares in that maner to some ignorant Christians. For he dare not so illude anie that knoweth that, neither can the spirite of the defunct returne to his friend, or yet an Angell vse such formes.

PHI. And are not our war-woolfes one sorte of these spirits also, that hauntes and troubles some houses or dwelling places?

EPI. There bath indeede bene an old opinion of such like thinges; For by the Greekes they were called {Greek lukanðrwpoi} which signifieth men-woolfes. But to tell you simplie my opinion in this, if anie such thing hath bene, I take it to haue proceeded but of a naturall super-abundance of Melancholie, which as wee reade, that it hath made some thinke themselues Pitchers, and some horses, and some one kinde of beast or other: So suppose I that it hath so viciat the imagination and memorie of some, as per lucida interualla, it hath so highlie occupyed them, that they haue thought themselues verrie Woolfes indeede at these times: and so haue counterfeited their actiones in goeing on their handes and feete, preassing to deuoure women and barnes, fighting and snatching with all the towne dogges, and in vsing such like other bruitish actiones, and so to become beastes by a strong apprehension, as Nebucad-netzar was seuen yeares:[1. Dan. 4.] but as to their hauing and hyding of their hard & schellie sloughes, I take that to be but eiked, by vncertaine report, the author of all lyes.

CHAP. II. ARGV.

The description of the next two kindes of Spirites, whereof the one followes outwardlie, the other possesses inwardlie the persones that they trouble. That since all Prophecies and visiones are nowe ceased, all spirites that appeares in these formes are euill.

PHILOMATHES.

COme forward now to the reste of these kindes of spirites.

EPI. As to the next two kindes. that is, either these that outwardlie troubles and followes some persones, or else inwardlie possesses them: I will conjoyne them in one, because aswel the causes ar alike in the persons that they are permitted to trouble: as also the waies whereby they may be remedied and cured.

PHI. What kinde of persones are they that vses to be so troubled?

EPI. Two kindes in speciall: Either such as being guiltie of greeuous offences, God punishes by that horrible kinde of scourdge, or else being persones of the beste nature peraduenture, that yee shall finde in all the Countrie about them, G O D permittes them to be troubled in that sort, for the tryall of their patience, and wakening vp of their zeale, for admonishing of the beholders, not to truste ouer much in themselues, since they are made of no better stuffe, and

64

peraduenture blotted with no smaller sinnes (as CHRIST saide, speaking of them vppon whome the Towre in Siloam fell:)[1. Luc. 13.] And for giuing likewise to the spectatators, matter to prayse G O D, that they meriting no better, are yet spared from being corrected in that fearefull forme.

PHI. These are good reasons for the parte of G O D, which apparantlie mooues him so to permit the Deuill to trouble such persones. But since the Deuil hath euer a contrarie respecte in all the actiones that G O D employes him in: which is I pray you the end and mark he shoots at in this turne?

EPI. It is to obtaine one of two thinges thereby, if he may: The one is the tinsell of their life, by inducing them to such perrilous places at such time as he either followes or possesses them, which may procure the same: And such like, so farre as G O D will permit him, by tormenting them to weaken their bodie, and caste them in incurable diseases. The other thinge that hee preases to obteine by troubling of them, is the tinsell of their Soule, by intising them to mistruste and blaspheme God: Either for the intollerablenesse of their tormentes, as he assayed to haue done with IOB;[1. Iob. x.] or else for his promising vnto them to leaue the troubling of them, incase they would so do, as is knowen by experience at this same time by the confession of a young one that was so troubled.

PHI. Since ye haue spoken now of both these kindes of spirites comprehending them in one: I must nowe goe backe againe in speering some questions of euerie one of these kindes in speciall. And first for these that followes certaine persones, yee know that there are two sortes of them: One sorte that troubles and tormentes the persones that they haunt with: An other sort that are seruiceable vnto them in all kinde of their necessaries, and omittes neuer to forwarne them of anie suddaine perrell that they are to be in. And so in this case, I would vnderstande whither both these sortes be but wicked and damned spirites: Or if the last sorte be rather Angells, (as should appeare by their actiones) sent by God to assist such as he speciallie fauoures. For it is written in the Scriptures, that God sendes Legions of Angells to guarde and watch ouer his elect.[2. Gen. 32. 1. Kin. 6 Psal. 34.]

EPI. I know well inough where fra that errour which ye alleage hath proceeded: For it was the ignorant Gentiles that were the fountaine thereof. Who for that they knew not God, they forged in their owne imaginationes, euery man to be still accompanied with two spirites, whereof they called the one genius bonus, the other genius malus: the Greekes called them {Greek endaimona} & {Greek kakodaimona}: wherof the former they saide, perswaded him to all the good he did: the other entised him to all the euill. But praised be God we that are christians, & walks not amongst the Cymmerian conjectures of man, knowes well inough, that it is the good spirite of God onely, who is the fountain of all goodnes, that perswads vs to the thinking or doing of any good: and that it is our corrupted fleshe and Sathan, that intiseth vs to the contrarie. And yet the Deuill for confirming in the heades of ignoraunt Christians, that errour first mainteined among the Gentiles, he whiles among the first kinde of spirits that I speak of, appeared in time of Papistrie and blindnesse, and haunted diuers houses, without doing any euill, but doing as it were necessarie turnes vp and down the house: and this spirit they called Brownie in our language, who appeared like a rough-man: yea, some were so blinded, as to beleeue that their house was all the sonsier, as they called it, that such spirites resorted there.

PHI. But since the Deuils intention in all his actions. is euer to do euill,, what euill was there in that forme of doing, since their actions outwardly were good.

EPI Was it not euill inough to deceiue simple ignorantes, in making them to take him for an Angell of light, and so to account of Gods enemie, as of their particular friend: where by the contrarie, all we that are Christians, ought assuredly to know that since the comming of Christ in the flesh, and establishing of his Church by the Apostles, all miracles, visions, prophecies, & appearances of Angels or good spirites are ceased. Which serued onely for the first sowing of faith, & planting of the Church. Where now the Church being established, and the white Horse whereof I spake before, hauing made his conqueste, the Lawe and Prophets are thought sufficient to serue vs, or make vs inexcusable, as Christ saith in his parable of Lazarus and the riche man.[1. Luk. 16.]

CHAP. III. ARGV.

The description of a particular sort of that kind of following spirites, called Incubi and Succubi: And what is the reason wherefore these kindes of spirites hauntes most the Northerne and barbarous partes of the world.

PHILOMATHES.

THE next question that I would speere, is likewise concerning this first of these two kindes of spirites that ye haue conjoyned: and it is this; ye knowe how it is commonly written and reported, that amongst the rest of the sortes of spirites that followes certaine persons, there is one more monstrous nor al the rest: in respect as it is alleaged, they converse naturally with them whom they trouble and hauntes with: and therefore I would knowe in two thinges your opinion herein: First if suche a thing can be: and next if it be: whether there be a difference of sexes amongst these spirites or not.

EPI. That abhominable kinde of the Deuils abusing of men or women, was called of old, Incubi and Succubi, according to the difference of the sexes that they conuersed with. By two meanes this great kinde of abuse might possibly be performed: The one, when the Deuill onelie as a spirite, and stealing out the sperme of a dead bodie, abuses them that way, they not graithlie seeing anie shape or feeling anie thing, but that which he so conuayes in that part: As we reade of a Monasterie of Nunnes which were burnt for their being that way abused. The other meane is when he borrowes a dead bodie and so visiblie, and as it seemes vnto them naturallie as a man converses with them. But it is to be noted, that in whatsoeuer way he vseth it, that sperme seemes intollerably cold to the person abused. For if he steale out the nature of a quick person, it cannot be so quicklie carryed, but it will both tine the strength and heate by the way, which it could neuer haue had for lacke of agitation, which in the time of procreation is the procurer & wakener vp of these two natural qualities. And if he occupying the dead bodie as his lodging expell the same out thereof in the dewe time, it must likewise be colde by the participation with the qualities of the dead bodie whereout of it comes. And whereas yee inquire if these spirites be diuided in sexes or not, I thinke the rules of Philosophie may easelie resolue a man of the contrarie: For it is a sure principle of that arte, that nothing can be diuided in sexes, except such liuing bodies as must haue a naturall seede to genere by. But we know spirites hath no seede proper to themselues, nor yet can they gender one with an other.

PHI. How is it then that they say sundrie monsters haue bene gotten by that way.

EPI. These tales are nothing but Aniles fabulæ. For that they haue no nature of their owne, I haue shewed you alreadie. And that the cold nature of a dead bodie, can woorke nothing in generation, it is more nor plaine, as being already dead of it selfe as well as the rest of the bodie is, wanting the naturall heate, and such other naturall operation, as is necessarie for woorking that effect, and incase such a thing were possible (which were all utterly against all the rules of nature) it would bread no monster, but onely such a naturall of-spring, as would haue cummed betuixt that man or woman and that other abused person, in-case they both being aliue had had a doe with other. For the Deuilles parte therein, is but the naked carrying or expelling of that substance: And so it coulde not participate with no qualitie of the same. Indeede, it is possible to the craft of the Deuill to make a womans bellie to swel after he hath that way abused her, which he may do, either by steiring vp her own humor, or by herbes, as we see beggars daily doe. And when the time of her deliuery should come to make her thoil great doloures, like vnto that naturall course, and then subtillie to slippe in the Mid-wiues handes, stockes, stones, or some monstruous barne brought from some other place, but this is more reported and gessed at by others, nor beleeued by me.

PHI. But what is the cause that this kinde of abuse is thought to be most common in such wild partes of the worlde, as Lap-land, and Fin-land, or in our North Iles of Orknay and Schet-land.

EPI. Because where the Deuill findes greatest ignorance and barbaritie, there assayles he grosseliest, as I gaue you the reason wherefore there was moe Witches of women kinde nor men.

PHI. Can anie be so vnhappie as to giue their willing consent to the Deuilles vilde abusing them in this forme.

EPI. Yea, some of the Witches haue confessed, that he hath perswaded them to giue their willing consent thereunto, that he may thereby haue them feltred the sikarer in his snares; But as the other compelled sorte is to be pittied and prayed for, so is this most highlie to be punished and detested.

PHI. It is not the thing which we cal the Mare, which takes folkes sleeping in their bedds, a kinde of these spirites, whereof ye are speaking?

EPI. No, that is but a naturall sicknes, which the Mediciners hath giuen that name of Incubus vnto ab incubando, because it being a thicke fleume, falling into our breast vpon the harte, while we are sleeping, intercludes so our vitall spirites, and takes all power from vs, as maks vs think that there were some vnnaturall burden or spirite, lying vpon vs and holding vs downe.

CHAP. IIII. ARGV.

The description of the Dæmoniackes &possessed. By what reason the Papistes may haue power to cure them.

PHILOMATHES.

WEL, I haue told you now all my doubts, and ye haue satisfied me therein, concerning the first of these two kindes of spirites that ye haue conjoyned. Now I am to inquire onely two thinges at you concerning the last kinde, I meane the Dæmoniackes. The first is, whereby shal these possessed folks be discerned fra them that ar trubled with a natural Phrensie or Manie. The next is, how can it be that they can be remedied by the Papistes Church, whome wee counting as Hereticques, it should appeare that one Deuil should not cast out an other, for then would his kingdome be diuided in it selfe, as CHRIST said.[1. Mat. 12 Mark. 3]

EPI. As to your first question; there are diuers symptomes, whereby that heauie trouble may be discerned from a naturall sickenesse, and speciallie three, omitting the diuers vaine signes that the Papistes attributes vnto it: Such as the raging at holie water, their fleeing a back from the Croce, their not abiding the hearing of God named, and innumerable such like vaine thinges that were alike fashious and feckles to recite. But to come to these three symptomes then, whereof I spake, I account the one of them to be the incredible strength of the possessed creature, which will farre exceede the strength of six of the wightest and wodest of any other men that are not so troubled. The next is the boldning vp so far of the patients breast and bellie, with such an vnnaturall sturring and vehement agitation within them: And such an ironie hardnes of his sinnowes so stiffelie bended out, that it were not possible to prick out as it were the skinne of anie other person so far: so mightely works the Deuil in all the members and senses of his body, he being locallie within the same, suppose of his Soule and affectiones thereof, hee haue no more power then of any other mans. The last is, the speaking of sundrie languages, which the patient is knowen by them that were acquainte with him neuer to haue learned, and that with an vncouth and hollowe voice, and al the time of his speaking, a greater motion being in his breast then in his mouth. But fra this last symptome is excepted such, as are altogether in the time of their possessing bereft of al their senses being possessed with a dumme and blynde spirite, whereof Christ releiued one, in the 12. Of Mathew. And as to your next demande, it is first to be doubted if the Papistes or anie not professing the the onelie true Religion, can relieue anie of that trouble. And next, in-case they can, vpon what respectes it is possible vnto them. As to the former vpon two reasons, it is grounded: first that it is knowen so manie of them to bee counterfite, which wyle the Clergie inuentes for confirming of their rotten Religion. The next is, that by experience we finde that few, who are possessed indeede, are fullie cured by them: but rather the Deuill is content to release the bodelie hurting of them, for a shorte space, thereby to obteine the perpetual hurt of the soules of so many that by these false miracles may be induced or confirmed in the profession of that erroneous Religion: euen as I told you before that he doth in the false cures, or casting off of diseases by Witches. As to the other part of the argument in-case they can, which rather (with reuerence of the learned thinking otherwaies) I am induced to beleeue, by reason of the faithfull report that men sound of religion, haue made according to their sight thereof, I think if so be, I say these may be the respectes, whereupon the Papistes may haue that power. CHRIST gaue a commission and power to his Apostles to cast out Deuilles, which they according thereunto put in execution: The rules he had them obserue in that action, was fasting and praier: & the action it selfe to be done in his name. This power of theirs proceeded not then of anie vertue in them, but onely in him who directed them. As was clearly proued by Iudas his hauing as greate power in that commission, as anie of the reste.

72

It is easie then to be vnderstand that the casting out of Deuilles, is by the vertue of fasting and prayer, and in-calling of the name of God, suppose manie imperfectiones be in the person that is the instrumente, as CHRIST him selfe teacheth vs of the power that false Prophets sall haue to caste out Devils.[1. Mat. 7.] It is no wounder then, these respects of this action being considered, that it may be possible to the Papistes, though erring in sundrie points of Religion to accomplish this, if they vse the right forme prescribed by CHRIST herein. For what the worse is that action that they erre in other thinges, more then their Baptisme is the worse that they erre in the other Sacrament, and haue eiked many vaine freittes to the Baptisme it selfe.

PHI. Surelie it is no little wonder that God should permit the bodies of anie of the faithfull to be so dishonoured, as to be a dwelling place to that vncleane spirite.

EPI. There is it which I told right now, would prooue and strengthen my argument of the deuils entring in the dead bodies of the faithfull. For if he is permitted to enter in their liuing bodies, euen when they are ioyned with the soule: how much more will God permit him to enter in their dead carions, which is no more man, but the filthie and corruptible caise of man. For as CHRIST Sayth, It is not any thing that enters within man that defiles him, but onely that which proceedes and commeth out of him.[1. Mark. 7]

CHAP. V. ARGV.

The description of the fourth kinde of Spirites called the Phairie: What is possible therein, and what is but illusiones.

73

How far this Dialogue entreates of all these thinges, and to
what end.

PHILOMATHES.

NOW I pray you come on to that fourth kinde of spirites.

EPI. That fourth kinde of spirites, which by the Gentiles was
called Diana, and her wandring Court, and amongst vs was
called the Phairie (as I tould you) or our good neighboures, was
one of the sortes of illusiones that was rifest in the time of
Papistrie: for although it was holden odious to Prophesie by the
deuill, yet whome these kinde of Spirites carryed awaie, and
informed, they were thought to be sonsiest and of best life. To
speake of the many vaine trattles founded vpon that illusion:
How there was a King and Queene of Phairie, of such a iolly
court & train as they had, how they had a teynd, & dutie, as it
were, of all goods: how they naturallie rode and went, eate and
drank, and did all other actiones like naturall men and women:
I thinke it liker VIRGILS Campi Elysij, nor anie thing that
ought to be beleeued by Christians, except in generall, that as I
spake sundrie times before, the deuil illuded the senses of
sundry simple creatures, in making them beleeue that they saw
and harde such thinges as were nothing so indeed.

PHI. But how can it be then, that sundrie Witches haue gone to
death with that confession, that they haue ben transported with
the Phairie to such a hill, which opening, they went in, and
there saw a faire Queene, who being now lighter, gaue them a
stone that had sundrie vertues, which at sundrie times hath
bene produced in judgement?

EPI. I say that, euen as I said before of that imaginar rauishing of the spirite foorth of the bodie. For may not the deuil object to their fantasie, their senses being dulled, and as it were a sleepe, such hilles & houses within them, such glistering courts and traines, and whatsoeuer such like wherewith he pleaseth to delude them. And in the meane time their bodies being senselesse, to conuay in their hande any stone or such like thing, which he makes them to imagine to haue receiued in such a place.

PHI. But what say ye to their fore-telling the death of sundrie persones, whome they alleage to haue seene in these places? That is, a sooth-dreame (as they say) since they see it walking.

EPI. I thinke that either they haue not bene sharply inough examined, that gaue so blunt a reason for their Prophesie, or otherwaies, I thinke it likewise as possible that the Deuill may prophesie to them when he deceiues their imaginationes in that sorte, as well as when he plainely speakes vnto them at other times for their prophesying, is but by a kinde of vision, as it were, wherein he commonly counterfeits God among the Ethnicks, as I told you before.

PHI. I would know now whether these kindes of spirites may only appeare to Witches, or if they may also appeare to anie other.

EPI. They may do to both, to the innocent sort, either to affraie them, or to seeme to be a better sorte of folkes nor vncleane spirites are, and to the Witches, to be a cullour of safetie for them, that ignorant Magistrates may not punish them for it, as I told euen now. But as the one sorte, for being perforce troubled with them ought to be pittied, so ought the other sorte (who

75

may bee discerned by their taking vppon them to Prophesie by
them,) That sorte I say, ought as seuerely to be punished as any
other Witches, and rather the more, that that they goe
dissemblingly to woorke.

PHI. And what makes the spirites haue so different names from
others.

EPI. Euen the knauerie of that same deuil; who as hee illudes
the Necromancers with innumerable feyned names for him and
his angels, as in special, making Sathan, Beelzebub, & Lucifer,
to be three sundry spirites, where we finde the two former, but
diuers names giuen to the Prince of all the rebelling angels by
the Scripture. As by CHRIST, the Prince of all the Deuilles is
called, Beelzebub in that place, which I alleaged against the
power of any hereticques to cast out Deuils. By IOHN in the
Reuelation, the old tempter is called, Sathan the Prince of all
the euill angels. And the last, to wit, Lucifer, is but by allegorie
taken from the day Starre (so named in diuers places of the
Scriptures) because of his excellencie (I meane the Prince of
them) in his creation before his fall. Euen so I say he deceaues
the Witches, by attributing to himselfe diuers names: as if
euery diuers shape that he trans formes himselfe in, were a
diuers kinde of spirit.

PHI. But I haue hard many moe strange tales of this Phairie,
nor ye haue yet told me.

EPI. As well I do in that, as I did in all the rest of my discourse.
For because the ground of this conference of ours, proceeded
of your speering at me at our meeting, if there was such a thing
as Witches or spirites: And if they had any power: I therefore
haue framed my whole discours, only to proue that such things

are and may be, by such number of examples as I show to be possible by reason: & keepes me from dipping any further in playing the part of a Dictionarie, to tell what euer I haue read or harde in that purpose, which both would exceede fayth, and rather would seeme to teach such vnlawfull artes, nor to disallow and condemne them, as it is the duetie of all Christians to do.

CHAP. VI. ARGV.

Of the tryall and punishment of Witches. What sorte of accusation ought to be admitted against them. What is the cause of the increasing so far of their number in this age.

PHILOMATHES.

THEN To make an ende of our conference, since I see it drawes late, what forme of punishment thinke ye merites these Magicians and Witches? For I see that ye account them to be all alike guiltie?

EPI. They ought to be put to death according to the Law of God, the ciuill and imperial law, and municipall law of all Christian nations.

PHI. But what kinde of death I pray you?

EPI. It is commonly vsed by fire, but that is an indifferent thing to be vsed in euery cuntrie, according to the Law or custome thereof.

PHI. But ought no sexe, age nor ranck to be exempted?

EPI. None at al (being so vsed by the lawful Magistrate) for it is the highest poynt of Idolatrie, wherein no exception is admitted by the law of God.

PHI. Then bairnes may not be spared?

EPI. Yea, not a haire the lesse of my conclusion. For they are not that capable of reason as to practise such thinges. And for any being in company and not reueiling thereof, their lesse and ignorant age will no doubt excuse them.

PHI. I see ye condemne them all that are of the counsell of such craftes.

EPI. No doubt, for as I said, speaking of Magie, the consulters, trusters in, ouer-seers, interteiners or sturrers vp of these craftes-folkes, are equallie guiltie with themselues that are the practisers.

PHI. Whether may the Prince then, or supreame Magistrate, spare or ouer-see any that are guiltie of that craft? vpon som great respects knowen to him?

EPI. The Prince or Magistrate for further tryals cause, may continue the punishing of them such a certaine space as he thinkes conuenient: But in the end to spare the life, and not to strike when God bids strike, and so seuerelie punish in so odious a fault & treason against God, it is not only vnlawful, but doubtlesse no lesse sinne in that Magistrate, nor it was in SAVLES sparing of AGAG[1. 1. Sam. 15.]. And so comparable to the sin of Witch-craft it selfe, as SAMVELL alleaged at that time.

PHI. Surely then, I think since this crime ought to be so seuerely punished. Iudges ought to beware to condemne any, but such as they are sure are guiltie, neither should the clattering reporte of a carling serue in so weightie a case.

EPI. Iudges ought indeede to beware whome they condemne: For it is as great a crime (as SALOMON sayeth,) To condemne the innocent, as to let the guiltie escape free;[2. Pro. 17] neither ought the report of any one infamous person, be admitted for a sufficient proofe, which can stand of no law.

PHI. And what may a number then of guilty persons confessions, woork against one that is accused?

EPI. The assise must serue for interpretour of our law in that respect. But in my opinion, since in a mater of treason against the Prince, barnes or wiues, or neuer so diffamed persons, may of our law serue for sufficient witnesses and proofes. I thinke surely that by a far greater reason, such witnesses may be sufficient in matters of high treason against God: For who but Witches can be prooues, and so witnesses of the doings of Witches.

PHI. Indeed, I trow they wil be loath to put any honest man vpon their counsell. But what if they accuse folke to haue bene present at their Imaginar conuentiones in the spirite, when their bodies lyes sencelesse, as ye haue said.

EPI. I think they are not a haire the lesse guiltie: For the Deuill durst neuer haue borrowed their shaddow or similitude to that turne, if their consent had not bene at it: And the consent in these turnes is death of the law.

PHI. Then SAMVEL was a Witch: For the Deuill resembled his shape, and played his person in giuing response to SAVLE.

EPI. SAMVEL was dead aswell before that; and so none coulde slander him with medling in that vnlawfull arte. For the cause why, as I take it, that God will not permit Sathan to vse the shapes or similitudes of any innocent persones at such vnlawful times, is that God wil not permit that any innocent persons shalbe slandered with that vile defection: for then the deuil would find waies anew, to calumniate the best. And this we haue in proofe by them that are carryed with the Phairie, who neuer see the shaddowes of any in that courte, but of them that thereafter are tryed to haue bene brethren and sisters of that craft. And this was likewise proued by the co~fession of a young Lasse, troubled with spirites, laide on her by Witchcraft. That although shee saw the shapes of diuerse men & women troubling her, and naming the persons whom these shaddowes represents: yet neuer one of them are found to be innocent, but al clearely tried to be most guilty, & the most part of them confessing the same. And besides that, I think it hath ben seldome harde tell of, that any whome persones guiltie of that crime accused, as hauing knowen them to be their marrowes by eye-sight, and not by hear-say, but such as were so accused of Witch-craft. could not be clearely tryed vpon them, were at the least publickly knowen to be of a very euil life & reputation: so iealous is God I say, of the fame of them that are innocent in such causes. And besides that, there are two other good helpes that may be vsed for their trial: the one is the finding of their marke, and the trying the insensiblenes thereof. The other is their fleeting on the water: for as in a secret murther, if the deade carcase be at any time thereafter handled by the murtherer, it wil gush out of bloud, as if the blud wer crying to the heauen for reuenge of the murtherer. God hauing appoynted that secret super-naturall signe, for tryall of that secrete vnnaturall crime, so it appeares that God hath appoynted (for a super-naturall signe of the monstruous impietie of the Witches) that the water shal refuse to receiue them in her bosom, that haue shaken off them the sacred Water of Baptisme, and wilfullie refused the benefite thereof: No not so much as their eyes are able to shed teares (thretten and torture them as ye please) while first they repent (God not permitting them to dissemble their obstinacie in so horrible a crime) albeit the women kinde especially, be able other-waies to shed teares at euery light occasion when they will, yea, although it were dissemblingly like the Crocodiles.

PHI. Well, wee haue made this conference to last as long as leasure would permit: And to conclude then, since I am to take my leaue of you, I pray God to purge this Cuntrie of these diuellishe practises: for they were neuer so rife in these partes, as they are now.

EPI. I pray God that so be to. But the causes ar ouer manifest, that makes them to be so rife. For the greate wickednesse of the people on the one parte, procures this horrible defection, whereby God justlie punisheth sinne, by a greater iniquitie. And on the other part, the consummation of the worlde, and our deliuerance drawing neare, makes Sathan to rage the more in his instruments, knowing his kingdome to be so neare an ende. And so fare-well for this time.[1. Reuel. 2.]

FINIS.

Breinigsville, PA USA
18 April 2010
236364BV00005B/78/A